Great Explorations in Math and Science (GEMS) Project

The Lawrence Hall of Science (LHS) is a public science center on the University of California at Berkeley campus. LHS offers a full program of activities for the public, including films, lectures, special events, exhibits, classes and workshops. LHS is also a center for teacher education and curriculum research and development.

Over the years, LHS staff have developed a number of activities, assembly programs, classes and exhibits. These programs have proved to be successful at the Hall and should be useful to other science centers, museums, schools, and community groups. Grants from the A. W. Mellon Foundation and the Carnegie Corporation of New York have made possible the publication of these activities under the "Great Explorations in Math and Science" (GEMS) title.

Staff

Glenn T. Seaborg, Principal Investigator
Robert C. Knott, Administrator
Jacqueline Barber, Director

Contributing Authors

Jacqueline Barber
Katharine Barrett
David Buller
Fern Burch
Deborah Calhoon
Linda De Lucchi
Jean Echols
Alan Gould
Sue Jagoda
Robert C. Knott
Larry Malone
Gay Nichols
Cary I. Sneider
Elizabeth Stage
Jennifer Meux White

Lisa Haderlie Baker, Art Director
Carol Bevilacqua and Nona Pepino, Designers
Lincoln Bergman and Kay Fairwell, Editors
Joanne Birdsall, Production Coordinator
Richard Randall, Exhibit Consultant

Reviewers

We would like to thank the following educators who reviewed, tested, or coordinated the reviewing of GEMS materials in manuscript form. Their critical comments and recommendations contributed significantly to these GEMS publications. Their participation does not necessarily imply endorsement of the GEMS program.

ALASKA

Olyn Garfield*
Galena City School, Galena

ARIZONA

Bill Armistead
Moon Mountain School, Phoenix

Flo-Ann Barwick
Lookout Mountain School, Phoenix

Richard E. Clark*
Washington School District, Phoenix

Bob Heath
Roadrunner School, Phoenix

Edie Helledy
Manzanita School, Phoenix

Greg Jesberger
Maryland School, Phoenix

Mark Kauppila
Acacia School, Phoenix

Karen Lee
Moon Mountain School, Phoenix

George Lewis
John Jacobs School, Phoenix

John Little
Palo Verde School, Phoenix

Tom Lutz
Palo Verde School, Phoenix

Tim Maki
Cactus Wren School, Phoenix

Don Metzler
Moon Mountain School, Phoenix

John O'Daniel
John Jacobs School, Phoenix

Donna Pickering
Orangewood School, Phoenix

Brenda Pierce
Cholla School, Phoenix

Ken Redfield
Washington School, Phoenix

Jean Reinoehl
Alta Vista School, Phoenix

Liz Sandberg
Desert Foothills School, Phoenix

Sandy Stanley
Manzanita School, Phoenix

Charri Strong
Lookout Mountain School, Phoenix

Shirley Vojtko
Cholla School, Phoenix

CALIFORNIA

Bob Alpert*
Vista School, Albany

Karen Ardito
White Hill Junior High School, Fairfax

James Boulier
Dan Mini Elementary School, Vallejo

Susan Butsch
Albany Middle School, Albany

Susan Chan
Cornell School, Albany

Robin Davis
Albany Middle School, Albany

Claudia Hall
Horner Junior High School, Fremont

Dale Kerstad*
Cave Elementary School, Vallejo

Joanna Klaseen
Albany Middle School, Albany

Margaret Lacrampe
Sleepy Hollow School, Orinda

Linda McClanahan*
Horner Junior High School, Fremont

Tina Neivelt
Cave Elementary School, Vallejo

Neil Nelson
Cave Elementary School, Vallejo

Mark Piccillo
Frick Junior High School, Oakland

Cindy Plambeck
Albany Middle School, Albany

Susan Power
Albany Middle School, Albany

Carol Rutherford
Cave Elementary School, Vallejo

Jim Salak
Cave Elementary School, Vallejo

Rich Salisbury
Albany Middle School, Albany

Secondo Sarpieri*
Vallejo City Unified School District, Vallejo

Bob Shogren*
Albany Middle School, Albany

Theodore L. Smith
Frick Junior High School, Oakland

Kay Sorg
Albany Middle School, Albany

Bonnie Square
Cave Elementary School, Vallejo

Jack Thornton*
Dan Mini Elementary School, Vallejo

Alice Tolinder*
Vallejo City Unified School District, Vallejo

Pamela Zimmerman
Cornell School, Albany

KENTUCKY

Mary Artner
Adath Jeshurun Preschool, Louisville

Alice Atchley
Wheatley Elementary School, Louisville

Sandi Babbitz
Adath Jeshurun Preschool, Louisville

Phyl Breuer
Holy Spirit School, Louisville

Toni Davidson
Thomas Jefferson Middle School, Louisville

August Drufke
Museum of History and Science, Louisville

Riva Drutz
Adath Jeshurun Preschool, Louisville

Linda Erman
Adath Jeshurun Preschool, Louisville

Jennie Ewalt
Adath Jeshurun Preschool, Louisville

Sam Foster
Museum of History and Science, Louisville

Nancy Glaser
Thomas Jefferson Middle School, Louisville

Laura Hansen
Sacred Heart Model School, Louisville

Leo Harrison
Thomas Jefferson Middle School, Louisville

Muriel Johnson
Thomas Jefferson Middle School, Louisville

Pam Laveck
Sacred Heart Model School, Louisville

Amy S. Lowen*
Museum of History and Science, Louisville

Theresa H. Mattei*
Museum of History and Science, Louisville

Brad Matthews
Jefferson County Public Schools, Louisville

Cathy Maddox
Thomas Jefferson Middle School, Louisville

Sherrie Morgan
Prelude Preschool, Louisville

Sister Mary Mueller
Sacred Heart Model School, Louisville

Tony Peake
Brown School, Louisville

Ann Peterson
Adath Jeshurun Preschool, Louisville

Mike Plamp
Museum of History and Science, Louisville

John Record
Thomas Jefferson Middle School, Louisville

Susan Reigler
St. Francis High School, Louisville

Anne Renner
Wheatley Elementary School, Louisville

Ken Rosenbaum
Jefferson County Public Schools, Louisville

Edna Schoenbaechler
Museum of History and Science, Louisville

Melissa Shore
Museum of History and Science, Louisville

Joan Stewart
DuPont Manual Magnet School, Louisville

Jenna Stinson
Thomas Jefferson Middle School, Louisville

Dr. William M. Sudduth*
Museum of History and Science, Louisville

Larry Todd
Brown School, Louisville

Harriet Waldman
Adath Jeshurun Preschool, Louisville

Fife Scobie Wicks
Museum of History and Science, Louisville

August Zoeller
Museum of History and Science, Louisville

Doris Zoeller
Museum of History and Science, Louisville

MICHIGAN

Dave Bierenga
South Christian School, Kalamazoo

Edgar Bosch
South Christian School, Kalamazoo

Craig Brueck
Schoolcraft Middle School, Schoolcraft

Joann Dehring
Woodland Elementary School, Portage

Tina Echols
Lincoln Elementary School, Kalamazoo

Barbara Hannaford
Gagie School, Kalamazoo

Dr. Alonzo Hannaford*
Science and Mathematics Education Center
Western Michigan University, Kalamazoo

Rita Hayden*
Science and Mathematics Education Center
Western Michigan University, Kalamazoo

Mary Beth Hunter
Woodland Elementary School, Portage

BUZZING A HIVE

TEACHER'S GUIDE

Grades K–3
Modifications for Preschool and Kindergarten
are described on pages 73–87

Skills
Observing, Comparing, Matching, Communicating, Role-Playing

Concepts
Honeybee Structure, Pollen, Nectar, Beehive, Bee's Life Cycle,
Bee Enemies, Protection, Cooperation, Communication, Bee's Flight Pattern

Science Themes
Systems & Interactions, Models & Simulations, Stability, Patterns of Change,
Evolution, Structure, Energy, Matter, Diversity & Unity

Mathematics Strands
Number, Pattern

Nature of Science and Mathematics
Interdisciplinary, Cooperative Efforts, Creativity & Constraints,
Real-Life Applications, Science and Technology

Time
Six 60-minute sessions, one 15-minute session,
two 20-minute sessions

Jean C. Echols

LHS GEMS

Great Explorations in Math and Science (GEMS)
Lawrence Hall of Science
University of California at Berkeley

Illustrations
Lisa Haderlie Baker

Photographs

Elizabeth Curtis
Jadin Hawkins
Valerie Haymaker
Gerald Zager

Lawrence Hall of Science,
University of California, Berkeley, CA 94720

Publication was made possible by grants from the
A. W. Mellon Foundation and the Carnegie
Corporation of New York. GEMS also gratefully
acknowledges the contribution of word processing
equipment from Apple Computer, Inc. This support
does not imply responsibility for statements or views
expressed in publications of the Great Explorations in
Math and Science (GEMS) program.

International Standard Book Number: 0-924886-39-0

COMMENTS WELCOME

Great Explorations in Math and Science (GEMS) is
an ongoing curriculum development project.
GEMS Guides are revised periodically, to
incorporate teacher comments and new
approaches. We welcome your criticisms,
suggestions, helpful hints, and any anecdotes
about your experience presenting GEMS
activities. Your suggestions will be reviewed each
time a GEMS Guide is revised. Please send your
comments to: GEMS Revisions,
% Lawrence Hall of Science, University of
California, Berkeley, CA 94720.

Ruth James
Portage Central High School, Portage

Dr. Phillip T. Larsen★
Science and Mathematics Education Center
Western Michigan University, Kalamazoo

Gloria Lett★
Kalamazoo Public Schools, Kalamazoo

Roslyn Ludwig
Woodland Elementary School, Portage

David McDill
Harper Creek High School, Battle Creek

Everett McKee
Woodland Elementary School, Portage

Susie Merrill
Gagie School, Kalamazoo

Rick Omilian★
Science and Mathematics Education Center
Western Michigan University, Kalamazoo

Kathy Patton
Northeastern Elementary School, Kalamazoo

Rebecca Penney
Harper Creek High School, Battle Creek

Shirley Pickens
Schoolcraft Elementary School, Schoolcraft

Deb Ply
South Junior High School, Kalamazoo

Sue Schell
Gagie School, Kalamazoo

Sharon Schillaci
Schoolcraft Elementary School, Schoolcraft

Julie Schmidt
Gagie School, Kalamazoo

Joel Schuitema
Woodland Elementary School, Portage

Bev Wrubel
Woodland Elementary School, Portage

NEW YORK

Frances Bargamian
Trinity Elementary School, New Rochelle

Bob Broderick
Trinity Elementary School, New Rochelle

Richard Golden★
Webster Magnet Elementary School, New Rochelle

Tom Mullen
Jefferson Elementary School, New Rochelle

Edna Neita
George M. Davis Elementary School, New Rochelle

Sigrin Newell
Discovery Center, Albany

Eileen Paolicelli
Ward Elementary School, New Rochelle

Dr. John V. Pozzi★
City School District of New Rochelle, New Rochelle

John Russo
Ward Elementary School, New Rochelle

Bruce Seiden
Webster Magnet Elementary School, New Rochelle

David Selleck
Albert Leonard Junior High School, New Rochelle

Tina Sudak
Ward Elementary School, New Rochelle

Julia Taibi
George M. Davis Elementary School, New Rochelle

Rubye Vester
Columbus Elementary School, New Rochelle

Bruce Zeller
Isaac E. Young Junior High School, New Rochelle

NORTH CAROLINA

Jorge Escobar
North Carolina Museum of Life and Science, Durham

Ed Gray
Discovery Place, Charlotte

Sue Griswold
Discovery Place, Charlotte

Mike Jordan
Discovery Place, Charlotte

James D. Keighton★
North Carolina Museum of Life and Science, Durham

Paul Nicholson
North Carolina Museum of Life and Science, Durham

John Paschal
Discovery Place, Charlotte

Cathy Preiss
Discovery Place, Charlotte

Carol Sawyer
Discovery Place, Charlotte

Patricia J. Wainland★
Discovery Place, Charlotte

OHIO

A.M. Sarquis
Miami University, Middletown

OREGON

Christine Bellavita
Judy Cox
David Heil★
Shab Levy
Joanne McKinley
Catherine Mindolovich
Margaret Noone★
Jim Todd
Ann Towsley
Oregon Museum of Science and Industry

Oregon Museum of Science and Industry (OMSI) staff conducted trial tests at the following sites:
Berean Child Care Center, Portland
Grace Collins Memorial Center, Portland
Mary Rieke Talented and Gifted Center,
    Portland Public School District, Portland
Portland Community Center, Portland
Portland Community College, Portland
St. Vincent De Paul, Child Development
    Center, Portland
Salem Community School, Salem
Volunteers of America, Child Care Center,
    Portland

WASHINGTON

David Foss
Stuart Kendall
Dennis Schatz★
William C. Schmitt
David Taylor
Pacific Science Center, Seattle

FINLAND

Sture Björk
Åbo Akademi, Vasa

Arja Raade
Katajanokka Elementary School, Helsinki

Pirjo Tolvanen
Katajanokan Ala-Aste, Helsinki

Gloria Weng★
Katajanokka Elementary School, Helsinki

★Trial test coordinators

Contents

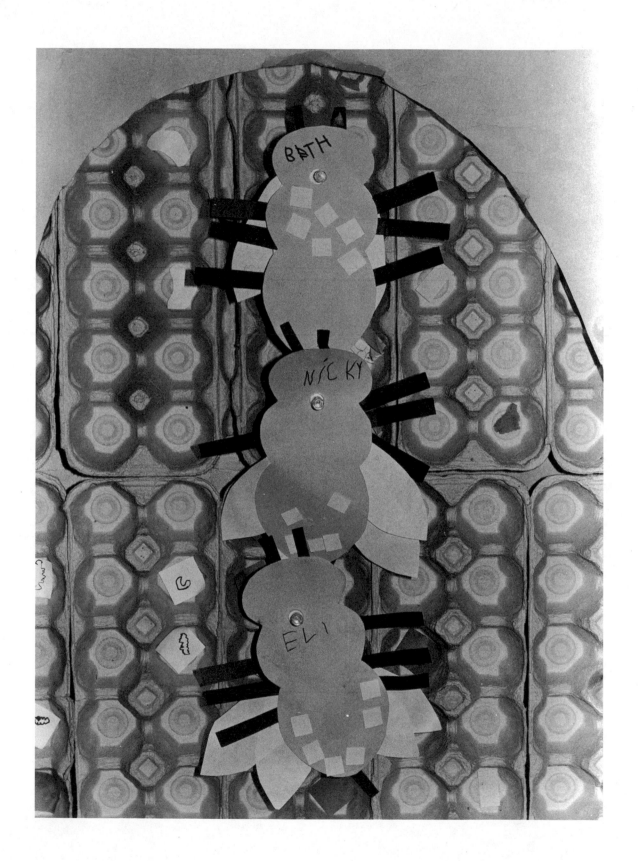

Acknowledgments

This activity was originated by Jean Echols in 1970. The author would like to thank Kimi Hosoume, Jane Callaway, Linda Coyle, Marion Buegler, Cathy Lampe, Valerie Haymaker, Melanie Yee, Darcy Struckman, and Kelly Kam for their advice and support during the further development and writing of *Buzzing a Hive* for publication as part of the GEMS series. Special thanks also goes to Jadin Hawkins and the children at Tehiyah School in El Cerrito, California.

There are many more people to acknowledge, but five stand out: my mother and my four children. When very young, my children could always find bees with full pollen baskets, which I would have passed unnoticed. Their enthusiasm for bees, along with my mother's support and encouragement, sparked my interest in developing *Buzzing a Hive*.

Introduction: Why Study Bees?

Most young children are fascinated by bees. Often their fascination is a mixture of fear and curiosity. Studying bees in class generates enthusiasm for these helpful insects and promotes a respect for bees and other living things.

Buzzing a Hive allows your students to explore the complexity of the honeybee's social behavior, communication, and hive environment. The children learn about bees by making paper bees, flowers with pollen, a beehive, and bee predators. They discover real pollen and nectar in flowers, and examine and taste honeycomb. During the last days of class, the children enact the drama of the beehive and perform bee dances.

Before Starting This Unit

It is important that you read "Behind the Scenes" on pages 69–71 before starting this unit. In addition to information on obtaining useful materials and setting up a mural, there is also a section concerning bee stings, in case you plan to have your students observe live bees. **However, no live bees are required for any of the activities in this unit.**

You may wish to write a letter home inquiring if any of your students have allergies to bee stings, or to pollen. The letter could also give a brief description of planned activities, which may help involve parents in discussing the activities with their children.

It is recommended that an assistant or parent volunteer help during this unit. You should also be advised that the time frames for each lesson are only approximations, and may vary considerably depending on class size and skill levels, familiarity with the topic, and length of discussion periods. Your own judgment and prior experience with the students can best determine appropriate time frames.

Age modifications for preschool and kindergarten children begin on page 73. First and second grade teachers may also be interested in reading this section, as it contains many useful suggestions.

In Lesson 2 you will be working with real flowers. To further involve your students, you may wish to plant nasturtiums as a class project a few months before you do the lesson, so you can use the flowers you planted.

A Different Way to Teach Science

Buzzing a Hive brings together many teaching approaches in a combination that allows children to learn science concepts through play, dramatics, role-playing, games, and art projects, as well as through observations, comparisons, and discussions. Toy animals and posters add visual stimulation. Using their senses, children discover for themselves some parts of the bee's real world: pollen, honey, and beeswax.

The short and varied activities reflect a step-by-step approach to teaching. Small bits of information are intermingled with physical activity. Questions are asked one at a time, to encourage time for thought and discussion. Questions focus children on the topic, help them recall previous information, or stimulate creative thinking. The question, "Why do you think bees make honey?" may evoke imaginative, delightful answers. You can accept fanciful responses as possibilities while guiding the children toward more logical answers.

Reinforcement of words and concepts with concrete examples and activities is an important part of this unit. The projects that the children make in class—bees, flowers, a hive, and predators—provide a creative way to record information and concepts. Seeing their projects on the class mural, playing with them at home, and sharing them with family and friends remind the children of the ideas introduced in class. These experiences extend the learning process and renew the interest generated in class.

New ideas and new words are repeated in a variety of ways. For example, children experience pollen gathering by role-playing bees gathering pollen, performing bee dances, and gluing pollen baskets to the paper bees' back legs. Each time the children repeat the pollen-gathering process, the concept and vocabulary are reinforced.

Buzzing a Hive is a progression of activities that reinforces as it builds. The mural is a visual expression of this progression. During each class, the children add something new to the mural. Excitement builds as the mural grows and bee mysteries unfold.

Winnie-the-Pooh sat down at the foot of the tree, put his head between his paws and began to think...

"That buzzing-noise means something. You don't get a buzzing-noise like that, just buzzing and buzzing, without its meaning something. If there's a buzzing-noise, somebody's making a buzzing-noise, and the only reason for making a buzzing-noise that *I* know of is because you're a bee."

Lesson 1: The Honeybee

Overview

In this activity, your students explore the basic structure of the honeybee worker and discover that it consists of: three body sections, six legs, four wings, two antennae, five eyes, and one stinger. The children find out where the body parts are attached and discuss their functions. The students also make paper honeybees and place them in a paper sky.

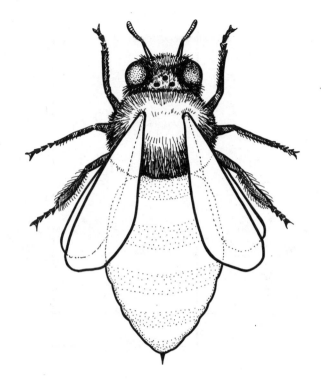

Time Frame

Observations	15 minutes
Teacher Demonstration	10 minutes
Children Make Paper Honeybees	25 minutes
Reflecting	10 minutes

What You Need

For a group of 32, including yourself:

- ☐ Construction paper (9″ x 12″ size) for paper bee:
  - _____ 5 sheets of yellow
  - _____ 9 sheets of white
  - _____ 2 sheets of black
- ☐ white paste or glue
- ☐ newspaper
- ☐ tray for demonstration
- ☐ blue paper for mural (about 18′ x 4′, see pages 70–71 for more details)
- ☐ 3 copies of "The Honeybee" poster (master included, page 13)

For each child and yourself:

- ☐ 1 copy of "The Honeybee" poster
- ☐ 1 pair of scissors
- ☐ 1 pencil

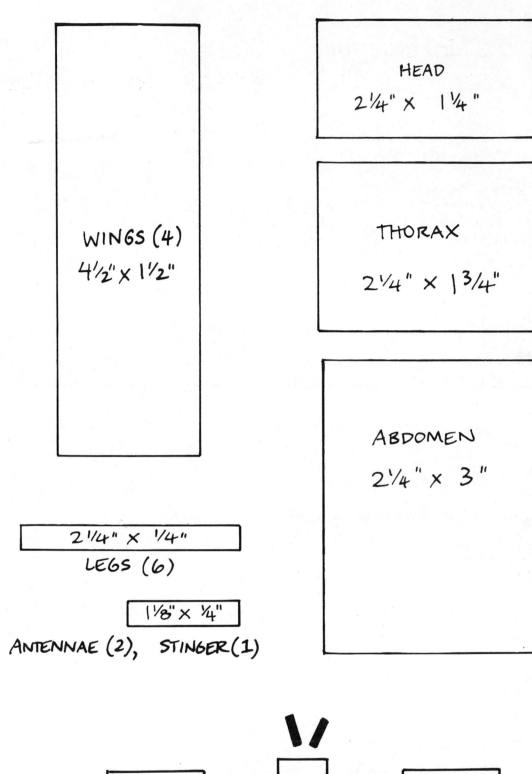

WINGS (4)
4½" × 1½"

HEAD
2¼" × 1¼"

THORAX
2¼" × 1¾"

ABDOMEN
2¼" × 3"

2¼" × ¼"
LEGS (6)

1⅛" × ¼"
ANTENNAE (2), STINGER (1)

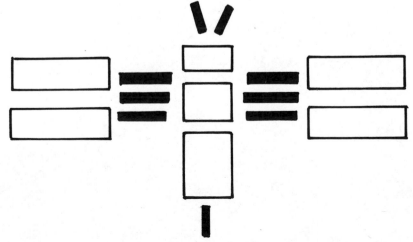

Getting Ready

1. Arrange for a parent volunteer or an assistant to help with the preparation and the class. (Assistance is recommended for all of the classes in this unit.)

2. Make one copy of "The Honeybee" poster for each child and for yourself. You will also need two or three extra copies for display.

3. Cut construction paper for paper bees. You and each child will need:

        ____ 3 yellow body sections
        ____ 4 white wing pieces
        ____ 6 black legs
        ____ 2 black antennae
        ____ 1 black stinger

Cut extra pieces of each.

4. If you plan to be working around live bees, contact a local health authority about emergency procedures in case a child is allergic to bee stings.

5. Carefully read the "Background For Teachers" section on page 89 and "Caution: Bee Stings" on page 70.

Setting Up The Room

Note: The following room organization is recommended for all the lessons in this unit:

1. Divide the room into a discussion area and a work area.

2. Arrange the discussion area so that the children will be able to see and participate in the demonstration and discussion.

3. It is best if you can lay the materials out on the tables or desks in the work area before the class comes in. When the children arrive, gather them in the discussion area to begin the day's activities.

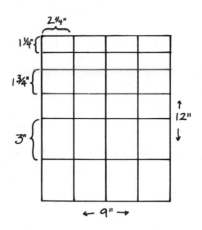

Helpful Hint

Cut eight sets of bee body sections out of one 9" x 12" sheet of paper. Cut four sheets at a time to make 32 sets of bee body sections. A paper cutter will help measuring and cutting go more quickly.

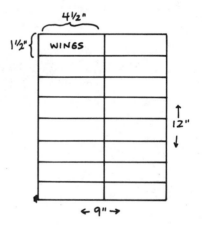

Cut 16 wings out of one 9" x 12" sheet of paper.

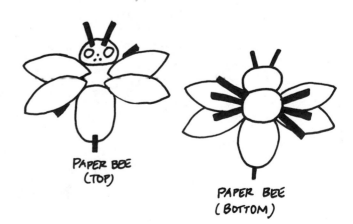

PAPER BEE (TOP)

PAPER BEE (BOTTOM)

The Work Area

1. Spread newspaper on the tables.

2. Place scissors, one pencil, paste, and three yellow rectangles at each child's work place.

3. Spread paper bee legs, stingers, antennae, and paper for wings on a table for the children to count.

4. Display several honeybee posters near the bee parts. The children can refer to the drawings if they have difficulty remembering the correct number of legs or wings.

The Discussion Area

Place in the discussion area:

1. A demonstration tray with newspaper, one pair of scissors, one pencil, and one container of paste. Also include paper pieces for constructing a bee and additional pieces to encourage the children to think about the correct number of bee body parts. These pieces include: six yellow construction paper rectangles for body sections (two large, two small, two middle-sized), nine black paper legs, seven white rectangles for wings, and four small black stinger and antennae pieces.

2. "The Honeybee" posters.

The Mural

Spread the blue paper for the mural on the floor near the discussion area.

Observations

1. Gather your students in the discussion area, and introduce the honeybee by showing the students "The Honeybee" poster. Allow time for the children to share their thoughts about bees. If necessary, begin the discussion with a few questions, such as:

- Where have you seen bees?

- What do they do?

- What do you like about bees?

- Have you ever been stung by a bee?

When the discussion turns to bee stings, have the children describe the sting and what they did to make it feel better.

2. Give each child a copy of "The Honeybee" poster.

3. Identify the main body sections (three ovals), using the words *head*, *thorax*, and *abdomen*. If the children are unfamiliar with these words, have them repeat the words after you.

4. Locate the bee's antennae. Ask, "Why do you think a bee needs antennae?" [For touch, smell, and possibly for hearing.]

5. Have the students count the legs (6), eyes (5), wings (4), stinger (1), antennae (2), and main body sections (3).

6. Ask questions that encourage careful observation, such as:

- To which body section do the legs connect? [Thorax.]

- Where are the wings attached? [Thorax.]

New Words:

thorax
abdomen
antennae (an-TEN-nee)
mural

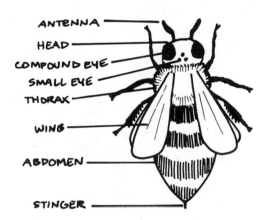

Teacher Demonstration

1. With your students in a half circle on the floor in front of the mural paper, tell them that they are going to make paper bees to place on the large sheet of blue paper. Show them the paper, and explain that the blue paper is the sky. The bees will be flying in the sky. Each day the children will add something new to the paper. It will become a huge picture or *mural*.

2. Spread six yellow construction paper rectangles in three different sizes in front of the children (as illustrated in Figure a).

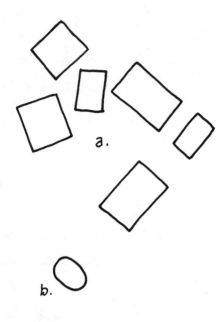
a.

3. Cut an oval body section out of one of the smallest rectangles (refer to Figure b).

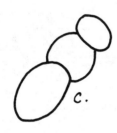
b.

4. Ask, "To make a bee, how many ovals will you need for body sections?" [Three.]

5. Cut a medium-sized and a large rectangle into ovals.

6. Have the students look at their bee posters. Ask, "Which body section is the largest?" [Abdomen.] "Which is the smallest?" [Head.] "Does anyone remember what the middle-size body section is called?" [Thorax.]

c.

7. Ask the students to look at the paper ovals and determine which is the head, thorax, and abdomen. Arrange the three ovals in a line from smallest to largest and glue them together (as illustrated in Figure c).

8. Pick up a black rectangle. Ask, "How many of these will you need for legs?" [Six.] "Where do the legs belong?" [On the thorax.] Glue the ends of the six legs to the thorax (as shown in Figure d).

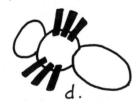
d.

9. Ask, "How many wings does a bee have?" [Four.] Cut out the wings and glue them to the thorax (as shown in Figure e).

Steps 9, 10, 11, and 12 do not have to be in this order. Ask, "What does the bee need now?" If a child says "stinger," start with #11. Let the children suggest the next step. However, it is important to glue the legs onto the thorax (step #8) before gluing on the wings.

10. Ask, "Where should we put the antennae?" [On the head.] Glue the two antennae to the bee's head. (See Figure f.)

11. Ask, "Where should we place the stinger?" [On the end of the abdomen.] Glue the stinger to the end of the abdomen. (See Figure f.)

12. Review the number of eyes a bee has. Draw five eyes on the honeybee. (See Figure g.)

13. To show the children where to write their names, write your name on the underside of the bee's head. (The abdomen and possibly the thorax will be covered up in a later activity.)

Children Make Paper Honeybees

1. Direct the students to the tables to cut out, arrange, and glue together the paper bee body sections. Tell the children to glue all the pieces to the top side of the bee so that the bee doesn't stick to the table.

2. Have the children count out the legs, glue them on the bee, and do the same with the other body pieces. If the children cannot remember how many legs or wings the bee has, refer them to the drawing.

3. Remind the students to write their names on the underside of the bee's head.

4. Have the children place their bees on the large sheet of blue paper (sky).

Reviewing

Bring the class together to review the number of bee body parts.

Going Further

1. Suggest that the children look for bees when they are outside playing; tell them to notice where they find the bees.

2. Caution the children to watch the bees without disturbing them.

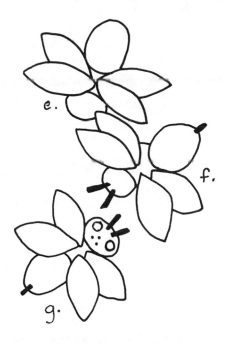

If you feel it is useful to have your students refer to the bee posters as they are gluing the bee parts together, have the children take their posters to their work area. Otherwise, they can put their posters away and refer to the ones on display as they are counting out the bee parts.

If children have difficulty cutting an oval shape, encourage them to snip off the corners of the rectangle.

Activity for a Learning Center

What You Need

For a group of six students:

- ☐ 6 dead bees (See page 69 for information on obtaining dead bees.)
- ☐ 6 cotton balls
- ☐ 1 egg carton
- ☐ 3 copies of "The Honeybee" poster
- ☐ 6 magnifying glasses (optional)

Getting Ready

1. Nest each dead bee on a cotton ball.

2. Place the cotton balls in the cups of an egg carton.

3. Spread the bee posters, magnifying glasses, and egg carton containing the dead bees on a table.

Observing Real Bees

1. Allow time for the children to pick up the cotton balls, observe the bees, and compare them with the bee posters.

2. After everyone has had a chance to observe the bees, ask questions that stimulate students to discuss the bees, such as:

- Did anyone see a stinger?

- Did your bee have all of its legs?

- Did you see any stripes on your bee?

For children who have never used a magnifying glass before, introduce the magnifying glasses first and allow time for practice. Have the children observe their hands and clothes under the magnifying glasses.

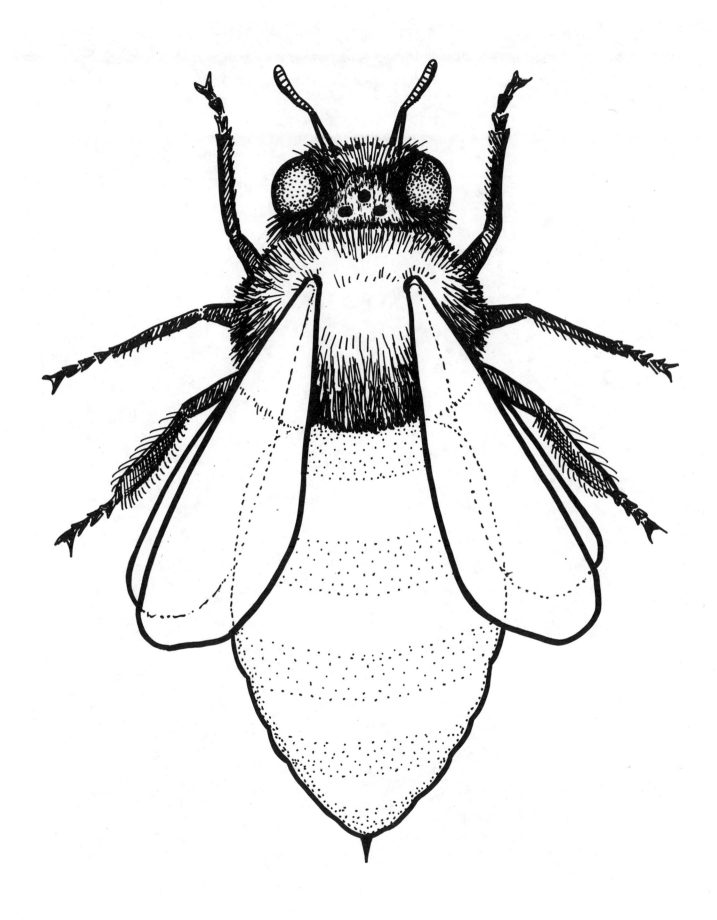

THE HONEYBEE

Lesson 2: Bees and Flowers, Pollen and Nectar

Overview

While pretending cotton balls are bees and rolling their "bees" around in real flowers, the children discover pollen in flowers. The students then learn how real bees collect pollen, carry it, and use it. The children make paper flowers that have pollen on the stamens, and place the flowers on the mural for their paper bees to visit.

In Session 2, students learn where bees find nectar to make honey. The children pretend they are bees, sipping pretend nectar with their straw proboscises.

Use of Real Flowers

During Session 1, your students will be working with real flowers. Be cautious, since many flowers are poisonous. The book *Know Your Poisonous Plants* is a helpful reference (see page 98). Also, find out if any of your students have asthma or pollen allergies.

In Session 2, children do **not** sip nectar from real flowers. Instead, they suck fruit juice with a straw. If the children were encouraged to taste nectar from nonpoisonous flowers in class, they might think it was all right to taste nectar from flowers found away from school, some of which might be poisonous.

Time Frame

Session 1: Pollen

Pollen Packers	20 minutes
Teacher Demonstration	10 minutes
Children Make Paper Flowers	30 minutes

Session 2: Nectar

Nectar Sippers	15 minutes
Reviewing	5 minutes

Session 1: Pollen

What You Need

For a group of 32, including yourself:

- [ ] colored construction paper (9″ x 12″) for flowers and grass:
    - _____ 32 sheets of white and/or orange
    - _____ 20 sheets of green
    - _____ 1 sheet of yellow
- [ ] white paste or glue
- [ ] "Bee Covered with Pollen" poster (master included, page 22)
- [ ] "Bee's Pollen Baskets" poster (master included, page 23)
- [ ] paper bees
- [ ] blue paper for mural
- [ ] 1 tray
- [ ] 1 trash can
- [ ] 4 or more containers for paper pollen and stamens, and for real flowers
- [ ] newspaper

For each child and yourself:

- [ ] 1 flower with pollen (see #1 in Getting Ready on this page)
- [ ] 1 cotton ball
- [ ] 1 pair of scissors
- [ ] 1 pencil

Getting Ready

1. Collect flowers heavy with yellow pollen, such as daisies and dahlias. If necessary, contact a local florist, botanical garden, or gardening center for information on non-poisonous flowers with large amounts of pollen. Optional: Inquire about flowers with blue, white, purple, orange, and/or red pollen.

2. Cut construction paper for grass and flowers. You and each child will need:

    ____ 1 sheet of orange or white, 9" x 12" (flower)
    ____ 4 pieces of yellow, 1" x ½" (pollen)
    ____ 1 piece of green, 12" x 1½" (stem)
    ____ 1 piece of green, 4" x 1½" (leaf)
    ____ 4 pieces of green, 2" x ½" (stamens)
    ____ 1 piece of green, 9" x 4" (grass)

3. Reread "Pollen and Nectar" on page 90.

Setting Up the Room

The Work Area

1. Spread newspaper on the tables.

2. Place paste, scissors, pencil, and paper for a flower (blossom, stem, and leaf) at each child's place.

3. Have paper for stamens, pollen, and grass set aside to distribute later.

The Discussion Area

Place in the discussion area:

1. A demonstration tray with newspaper, paste, scissors, pencil, paper for flower blossom (1), stem (1), leaf (1), grass (1), stamens (4), pollen (4), and a real flower.

2. Posters.

3. Flowers with pollen.

4. Cotton balls.

5. Trash can.

The Mural

1. Spread the large sheet of blue paper on the floor near the discussion area.

2. Place paper bees on the blue paper.

GO!

Pollen Packers

1. Gather the children in the discussion area and ask if any of them have ever seen bees on flowers. Ask, "What did you see them doing on the flowers?" Encourage their own observations, such as "looking at the flowers," "walking," "smelling the flowers," or "sipping nectar."

2. Distribute flowers with yellow pollen. (Or you may wish to have the flowers placed throughout the room, and have the children walk around the room collecting pollen.)

3. Pass a cotton ball to each child. Tell the children to pretend the cotton balls are bees. Say, "Roll your bee around in the flower and see what happens." (The cotton balls will quickly become covered with pollen.)

4. Ask the students if they know what the yellow dust is called. [Pollen.] Tell them that bees eat pollen.

5. Show your students the "Bee Covered with Pollen" poster.

6. Tell the children that the bee rolls around in the flower just as their cotton balls did. It then combs and scrapes its body, using its legs to clean off the pollen. The bee then packs the pollen between the long sturdy hairs on its back legs. These are called pollen baskets.

7. Show your students the "Bee's Pollen Baskets" poster, and tell them that bees carry pollen home in their pollen baskets.

New Words:

pollen
stamen

Teacher Demonstration

1. Tell the children that they are going to make paper flowers with pollen.

2. Identify parts of a large, real flower (petal, blossom, stem, leaf, stamen, and pollen on the stamen; see diagram).

3. Show the children how to make a flower (see drawing on this page, or, if you wish, use template on page 78). As you make each part, compare the paper parts with the parts of a real flower.

   a. Cut a flower blossom out of a sheet of construction paper

   b. Glue the stem to the blossom.

   c. Cut out a leaf and glue the leaf to the stem.

   d. Glue stamens on the blossom and pollen on the stamens.

4. Make grass by cutting snips into the top of a rectangular piece of green paper.

5. Glue the grass to the base of the flower.

Children Make Flowers

1. Tell the children to go to the tables and construct their flowers.

2. Remind them to write their names on the back of the flower blossoms.

3. Distribute the paper for stamens, pollen, and grass when your students are ready to add them to their flowers.

4. Have the children place (or tape) their flowers and grass on the large sheet of blue paper which is on the floor. (Do not use glue. Students will take their projects home at the end of the unit.)

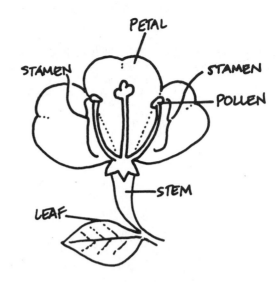

Your students can glue four or more stamens with pollen onto their flowers.

Going Further

If flowers with white, orange, red, blue, and/or purple pollen are readily available, bring them to class for the students to observe. African daisies have orange pollen. Gilia flowers have blue, and gladiolas have different shades of blue or purple pollen.

Session 2: Nectar

What You Need

For a group of 32, including yourself:

- ☐ "Bee's Proboscis" poster (master included, page 24)
- ☐ 4 trays
- ☐ 1 trash can
- ☐ 1 bottle or can of fruit juice, 64 oz. size
- ☐ 1 jar of honey, 8 oz. size
- ☐ 1 sheet of waxed paper (12" x 24")
- ☐ sponges for cleanup

For each child and yourself:

- ☐ 1 paper cup, 3 oz. size or larger
- ☐ 1 drinking straw cut in half to a length of about 4"
- ☐ 1 damp paper towel

Getting Ready

1. Cut the waxed paper into 3" squares.

2. Place a few drops of honey on each square, and put the waxed paper with honey on two trays.

3. Pour juice into cups and place the cups on trays.

4. Cut straws in half.

5. Set damp paper towels aside to distribute after the children taste the honey.

Nectar Sippers

1. Show your students the "Bee's Proboscis" poster. Ask, "What do you think a bee would do with a mouth shaped like a straw?" Allow time for the children to share their ideas.

2. Explain that bees suck a sweet juice called nectar from flowers, using a straw-like mouthpiece, called a proboscis. Have the children repeat the word, "proboscis" (pro-BOS-kiss) after you.

3. Ask, "Who wants to be a bee and sip a drop of nectar through a pretend proboscis (straw)?" Hand out straws and the paper cups containing juice. The children can pretend they are bees sipping nectar.

4. Tell the children that nectar is changed to honey in a special stomach, called a honey stomach.

5. Ask, "Why do you think bees make honey?" The children may say, "Because it tastes good" or "For us to eat." You can accept these responses as possibilities while telling your students that bees also eat honey.

6. Distribute the honey on small pieces of waxed paper for your students to taste.

Reviewing

Ask review questions, such as:

- Does anyone remember the name of the bee's mouthpiece? [Proboscis.]

- What does the bee take from the flowers to make honey? [Nectar.]

- What does the bee carry in its leg baskets? [Pollen.]

Going Further

Compare the "Bee's Proboscis" poster with pictures of the mouth parts of other animals that sip nectar, such as butterflies, hummingbirds, long-tongued bats and mosquitoes.

New Words:

nectar
proboscis (pro-BOS-kiss
or pro-BOS-sis)

BEE COVERED WITH POLLEN

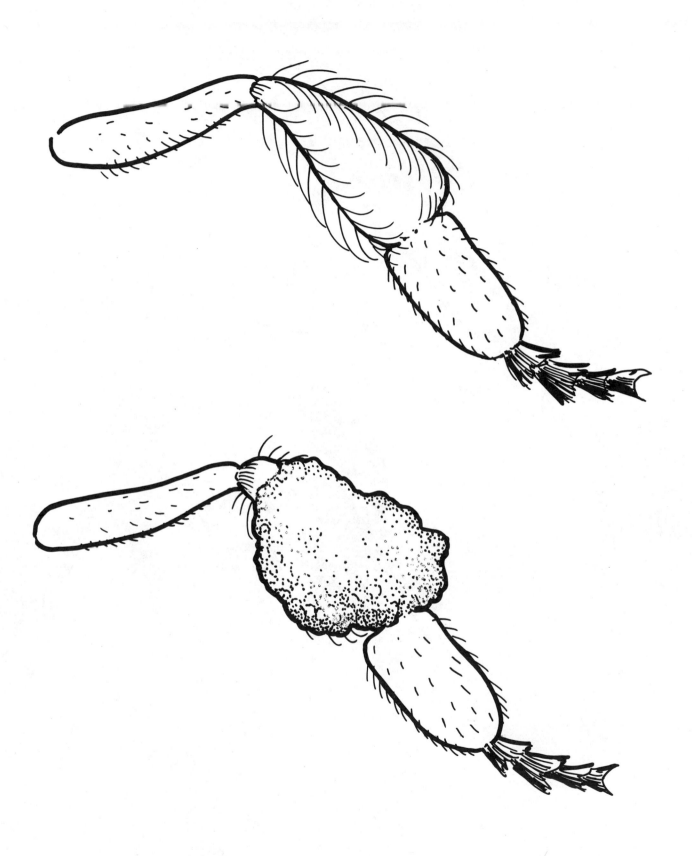

BEE'S POLLEN BASKETS

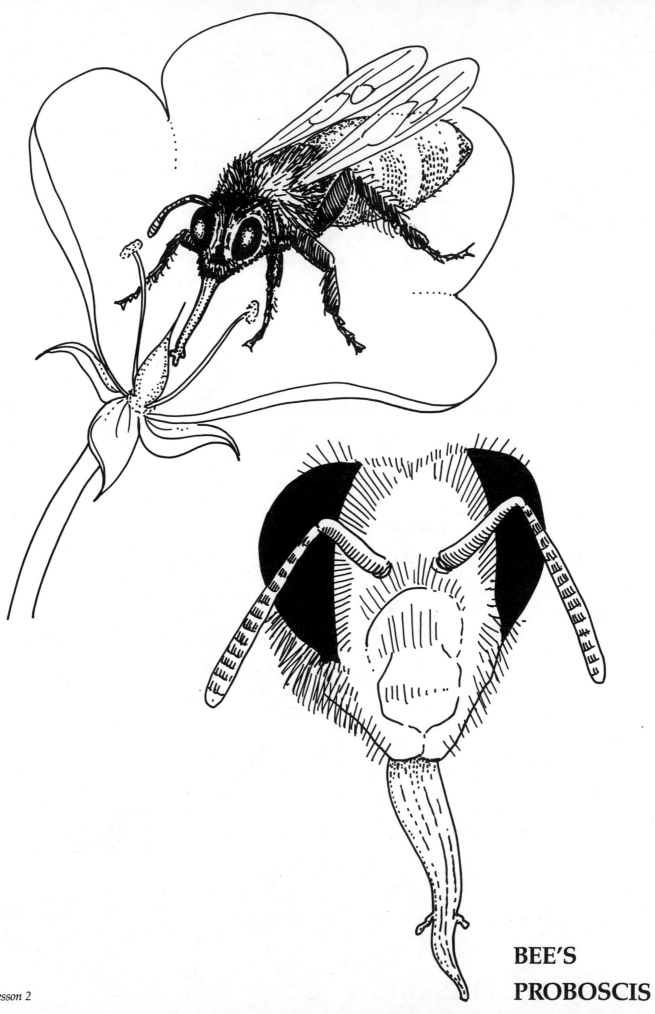

**BEE'S
PROBOSCIS**

Lesson 3: Building A Beehive

Overview

In this activity, students discover that honeycomb is made of wax. They learn where the wax comes from, and how the bees hang in chains while carefully and cooperatively making their honeycomb cells. The children give their paper bees wax scales, and then work together as a class to build a paper hive.

Time Frame

Discovering the Hive	10 minutes
Adding Wax Scales	20 minutes
Joining Bees in Building a Hive	20 minutes
Reflecting	10 minutes

What You Need

For a group of 32, including yourself:

- [ ] yellow, brown, or white butcher paper, approximately 8' x 3½' for a large hive
- [ ] 2 sheets of yellow construction paper (9" x 12" size) for adding wax scales
- [ ] 1 sheet of waxed paper (12" x 12")
- [ ] 1 large pair of scissors for cutting out the hive
- [ ] 1 chunk of wax
- [ ] other wax objects, such as birthday candles, crayons, and lipstick
- [ ] paper demonstration bee
- [ ] demonstration tray
- [ ] newspaper
- [ ] white paste or glue
- [ ] mural with bees and flowers
- [ ] "Beehives" poster (master included, page 33)
- [ ] "Inside the Hive" poster (master included, page 34)
- [ ] "Bee with Wax Scales" poster (master included, page 35)
- [ ] "Bees Hanging in Chains" poster (master included, page 36)
- [ ] several empty pieces of honeycomb (optional)

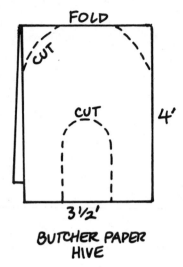

FOLD

CUT

CUT

4'

3½'

BUTCHER PAPER
HIVE

For each child and yourself:

☐ 1 paper egg carton, preferably yellow
☐ 1 pair of scissors
☐ 1 pencil

Getting Ready

1. You will need a group hive made of butcher paper to place on the mural. To make a hive, fold the 3½' x 8' paper in half. Cut an arched doorway. Cut off corners of the folded end. (See drawing.)

2. Cut paper for adding wax scales. You and each child will need:

_____ 1 piece yellow, 1½" x 2½" (underside of abdomen)

_____ 2 or more pieces of waxed paper, 1" x 1" (for wax scales)

3. Hide the remaining waxed paper with the other wax objects, for display later in the activity.

4. If the children in your class are skilled enough with scissors, have them cut the lids off the egg cartons, the slits for wax scales, and the wax scales. If not, do the cutting for them ahead of time. Note: Cutting waxed paper is more difficult than cutting construction paper. (For instructions explaining how to cut the wax scales and the slits, see "Adding Wax Scales," page 30.)

5. Reread "Beehives" on pages 91–92.

Setting Up The Room

The Work Area

1. Spread newspaper on the tables.

2. At each child's work area place a pencil, paste, a pair of scissors, two pieces of waxed paper, and one yellow rectangle.

The Discussion Area

Place in the discussion area:

1. A demonstration tray with newspaper, scissors, paste, pencil, yellow rectangle, one piece of waxed paper, one egg carton, and the paper demonstration bee.

2. Wax and wax objects (hidden).

3. Posters.

4. Egg cartons for the students.

5. Empty pieces of honeycomb (optional).

The Mural

1. Spread the mural with flowers and bees on the floor. (Students will remove the bees for a class activity.)

2. Do not attach the large hive to the mural until after the next lesson, "What's in a Hive?" The hive will be used in the demonstration circle for two activities, "Joining Bees in Building a Hive," pages 30–32, and "Young Bees Drama," pages 47–48.

GO!

Discovering the Hive

1. Tell the children that many animals like the taste of honey. Ask, "Do any of you know where bees hide their honey?" [Beehive.] Let the children share what they know about beehives.

2. Show the "Beehives" and "Inside the Hive" posters. Point out the honeycomb inside the hive.

Optional: If you obtained small empty pieces of honeycomb, pass them around so the children can touch the wax and feel how light it is.

3. Explain that the small, empty spaces in the honeycomb are called cells. Ask, "Do any of you know what these cells are made of?" [Wax.]

4. Hold up a chunk of wax. Ask, "What do people make out of wax?" Bring candles, crayons, lipstick, and waxed paper out of hiding as the children name them. Give a few hints if students cannot think of wax objects.

New Words:

beehive
honeycomb
cell
wax scales

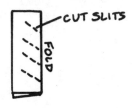

CUT SLITS
FOLD

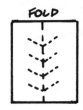

FOLD

WAX SCALE

WAXED PAPER

WAX SCALE

Adding Wax Scales

1. Show the "Bee With Wax Scales" poster. Tell the children that bees make their own wax. Explain that wax comes out of the bee's body in small pieces called wax scales. Point to the wax scales on the poster and ask, "On which body section do you see the wax scales? [Abdomen.] Say, "Let's give our paper bees wax scales."

2. Show the children how to make a bee with wax scales.

   a. Fold the 1½" x 2½" piece of yellow construction paper in half lengthwise.

   b. Cut four slits on the folded edge.

   c. Unfold.

   d. Apply glue **along the edges** away from slits.

   e. Glue the rectangle to the underside of bee's abdomen.

   f. Cut the 1" square of waxed paper into quarters to represent wax scales.

   g. Insert wax scales into slits. You should be able to remove the scales from the abdomen. (See drawing).

3. Have the children collect their bees from the mural and take them to the work area.

4. Have the children add the scales to their bees, giving step-by-step instructions if necessary.

Joining Bees in Building a Hive

1. Instruct the students to bring their paper bees to the discussion area, and arrange the bees in straight lines on the floor in the middle of the circle, with the wax scales showing.

2. Display the "Bees Hanging in Chains" poster.

3. Explain that when bees are making wax to build a hive, they hang in chains—holding on to each other with their feet. Hanging stretches their bodies and lets the wax ooze out.

4. Have the children pretend that their bees are hanging in chains. You may want to point out that in real life, the hive is standing up. Therefore, the bees would actually be hanging, not lying flat on the floor. To demonstrate, hold up three bees in a hanging position.

5. Suggest that the class join the bees in building a hive.

   a. Hold up an open egg carton. Say, "Let's pretend that these are cells a paper bee made."

   b. Cut the lid off the carton.

   c. Show your students where to write their names by writing your name on the side of the egg carton.

   d. Hold up the bee that is at the end of the chain closest to you. Explain that when a bee is building a hive, it removes the wax scales from its abdomen, and places them on a cell in the hive. Remove a scale from the paper bee.

   e. Glue one or two paper scales to an egg carton cell.

6. Pass out egg cartons or have the children pick them up on their way to the work area.

Some students may have difficulty writing their names on the egg cartons. In this case, have them write their names on scraps of paper and glue the paper to the carton.

7. Instruct the children to build cells for a hive, giving step-by-step instructions if necessary.

    a. Cut lids off egg cartons.

    b. Write names on cartons.

    c. Get paper bees from chains in circle.

    d. Have paper bees pull out wax scales.

    e. Glue scales to egg carton cells.

8. Spread out the large paper hive in the middle of the circle in the discussion area. As the children finish building their cells, have them place their cells and bees inside the hive. Tell the children that many bees work together to build wax cells, and that is how their home is built.

9. Ask your students not to glue or tape the cells to the hive because in the next session they will remove their cells from the hive in order to fill them. They will learn what bees put in the cells.

Reflecting

As the children are sitting around the paper hive, spend a few minutes sharing thoughts about beehives. Ask, "What surprised you about a beehive?"

Going Further

Ask your students to see how many things they and their families can find around the house that are made of wax, and have the children bring the wax objects to school to share. The class could set up a display area of wax objects.

Straw Hive

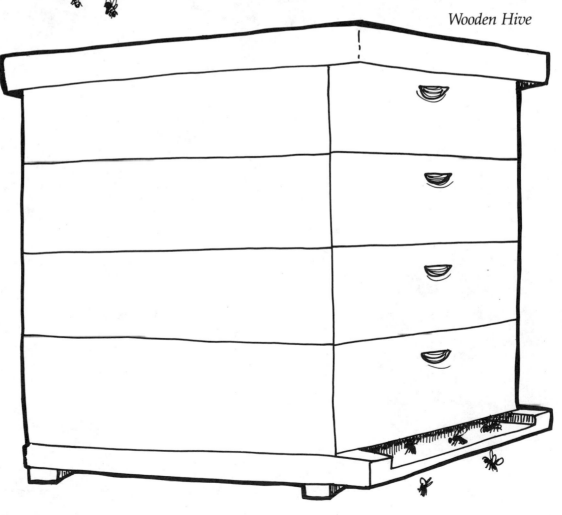

Wooden Hive

BEEHIVES

INSIDE
THE HIVE

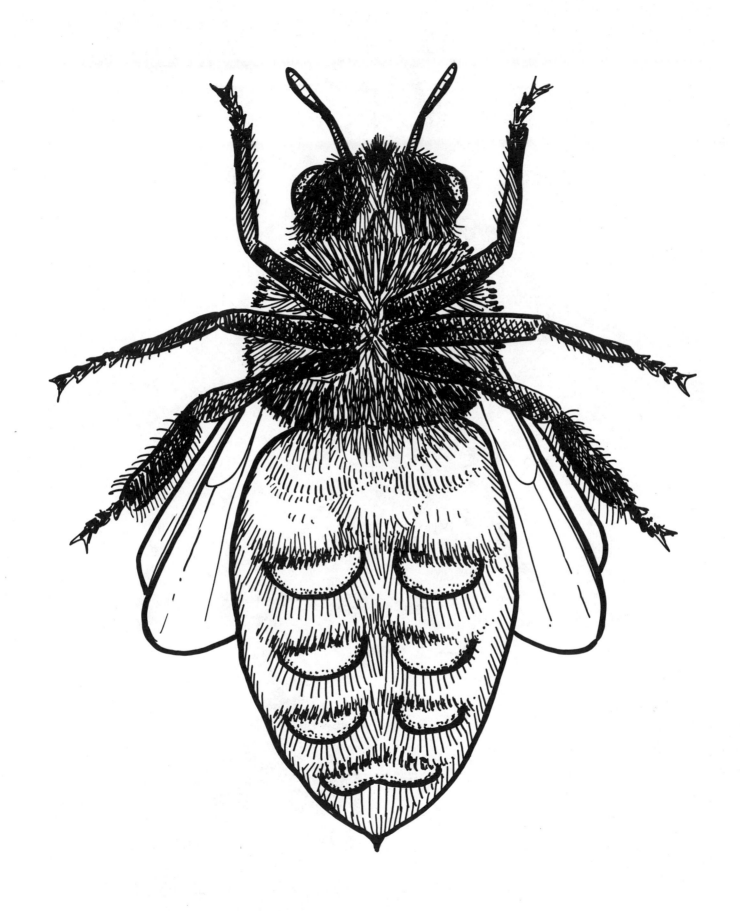

BEE WITH WAX SCALES

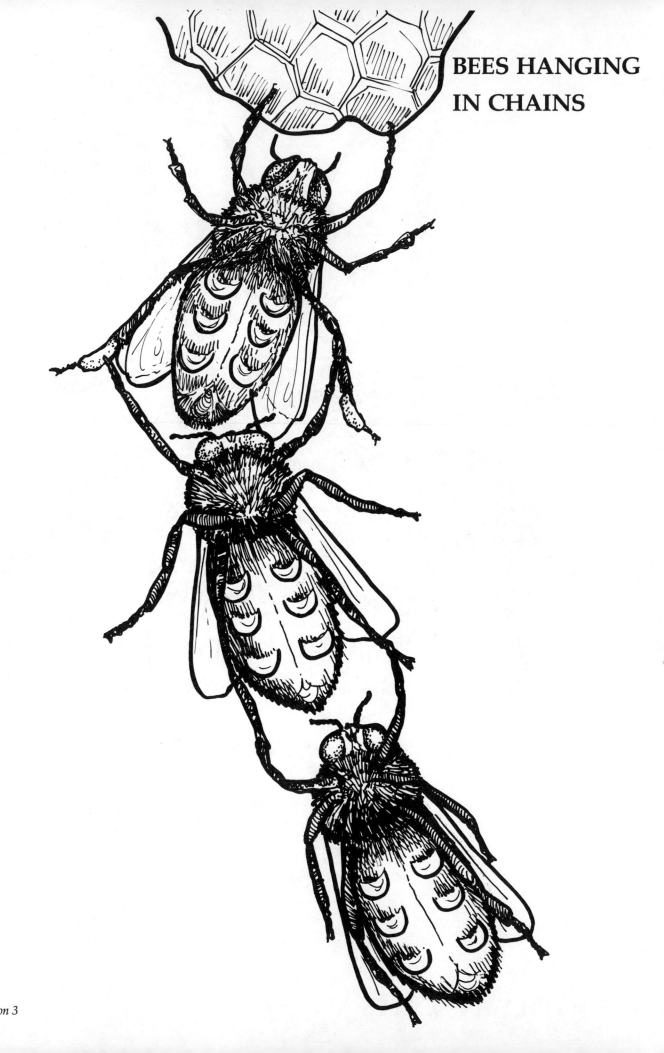

**BEES HANGING
IN CHAINS**

Lesson 4: What's In A Hive?

Overview

What goes on inside a honeybee hive? In this lesson, children learn that the hive is a place where food is stored, eggs are laid, and young bees experience incredible changes, both in appearance and in the variety of jobs they perform. Students find out what is hidden in a hive as they taste honeycomb and then glue paper pollen, honey, eggs, larvae, and pupae into the cells of their paper hive.

Students also study the early stages in the life cycle of the bee by observing and comparing posters of larvae and pupae, and by role-playing nurse bees feeding larvae. During the last session of the class, children use the paper bees they made to enact the drama of young bees at work inside a honeybee hive, while older bees in the field gather food to store in the hive.

Time Frame

Session 1: Exploring Honeycomb   15 minutes

Session 2: The Queen Bee and Her Babies

The Queen Bee	5 minutes
Baby Bees and Nurse Bees	15 minutes
Change to Adult Bee	10 minutes
Teacher Demonstration	10 minutes
Children Fill Their Egg Carton Cells	20 minutes

Session 3: Young Bees Drama   20 minutes

Session 1: Exploring Honeycomb

What You Need

For a group of 32, including yourself:

- ☐ 1 8-oz. package of honey in the comb (available in many health food stores)
- ☐ 1 sheet of waxed paper (12″ x 24″)
- ☐ 1 paper plate
- ☐ 1 trash can
- ☐ 2 or 3 sponges
- ☐ 3 trays

For each child and yourself:

- ☐ 1 damp paper towel

Getting Ready

1. Cut the waxed paper into 3″ squares.

2. Cut a very small piece of honeycomb for each child. Put the honeycomb pieces on the waxed paper squares. Place the damp towels and waxed paper with honeycomb on the trays. Place the remaining honeycomb on the paper plate.

GO!

Exploring Honeycomb

1. As a review, ask if anyone in the class remembers what the cells in the honeycomb are made of. [Wax.] Introduce the real honeycomb by saying, "Let's find out what bees put in the wax cells."

2. Pass the uncut honeycomb around so the students can observe the wax cells filled with honey. Point out how the bees use wax to cap the cells for storage.

3. Distribute small pieces of honeycomb on pieces of waxed paper for the children to taste.

It is safe to eat the wax.

Session 2: The Queen Bee and Her Babies

What You Need

For a group of 32, including yourself:

- [ ] construction paper (9″ x 12″) for queen bee:
  - ____ ¼ sheet of white, 6″ x 4½″
  - ____ ¼ sheet of yellow, 3″ x 9″
  - ____ ¹⁄₁₆ sheet of black, 2¼″ x 3″
- [ ] construction paper (9″ x 12″) for pollen, honey, eggs, larvae, and pupae:
  - ____ 2 sheets of yellow
  - ____ 2 sheets of brown
  - ____ 2 sheets of white
- [ ] "The Queen Bee and Her Eggs" poster (master included, page 50)
- [ ] "The Larvae" poster (master included, page 51)
- [ ] "The Pupae" poster (master included, page 52)
- [ ] demonstration bee
- [ ] paper hive with egg carton cells inside
- [ ] white paste or glue
- [ ] newspaper
- [ ] 3 trays
- [ ] 34 3-oz. paper cups
- [ ] 1 8-oz. jar of honey (same jar used in Lesson 2)
- [ ] 4 graham crackers
- [ ] 1 small bag (plastic or paper)
- [ ] 1 sponge
- [ ] 1 trash can

For each child and yourself:

- [ ] 1 pencil
- [ ] 1 pair of scissors
- [ ] 1 drinking straw cut in half to a length of about 4″

Getting Ready

1. Make a queen bee. (See illustration and pattern.)

    a. Cut construction paper for queen bee:
  - ____ 3 yellow body sections
  - ____ 6 black legs
  - ____ 2 black antennae
  - ____ 1 black stinger
  - ____ 4 white wing pieces

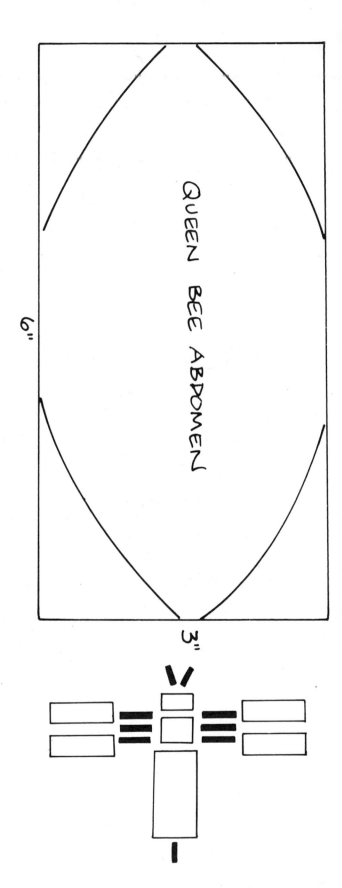

6″

3″

QUEEN BEE ABDOMEN

The proportions for the queen bee are the same as those for the worker bee (see page 6) except the queen's abdomen is larger.

b. Cut body sections and wings into ovals. Glue the body sections together, and add six legs, four wings, two antennae, and one stinger.

c. Draw five eyes.

2. Cut construction paper for pollen, honey, eggs, larvae, and pupae into 2" squares. You and each child will need one square of each of the following colors:
_____ yellow (pollen)
_____ brown (honey)
_____ white (eggs, larvae, and pupae)

Cut extra pieces. Some children may want more.

3. Prepare two pretend honeycomb trays. Pour about ⅛" of honey into a cup for each child and for yourself. Place the cups on the trays. To make pretend pollen, put the graham crackers in a small bag and break them into fine crumbs. Pour the crumbs into two cups, and place one cup of pretend pollen on each tray.

4. Cut the straws in half.

5. Reread "Bee Metamorphosis and Diet" on page 92.

Setting Up The Room

The Work Area

1. Spread newspaper on the tables.

2. Arrange the following items at each child's work place: one piece of brown paper (honey), one piece of yellow paper (pollen), one piece of white paper (eggs, larvae, pupae), a pencil, paste, and scissors.

The Discussion Area

Place in the discussion area:

1. A demonstration tray with newspaper, egg carton, one piece each of white, brown, and yellow paper, a pencil, paste, and scissors.

Caution: Pollen

Although real pollen can be purchased from a health food store, it is recommended that crumbled graham crackers be used as pretend pollen. Eating real pollen in class might give a child the impression that it is all right to eat pollen from a flower away from school, and that flower may be poisonous. Also, some individuals have severe allergic reactions to pollen.

2. Posters.

3. Trash can and sponge for cleanup.

The Large Hive

Place the paper hive flat on the floor in the discussion area. Have the egg carton cells in the hive. Hide the queen bee and demonstration bee inside the hive.

The Queen Bee

1. Gather your students in the discussion area.

2. Ask, "What do bees hide in the wax cells inside the hive?" [Honey.] Tell the children that tiny eggs are also hidden in the cells.

3. Ask, "Does anyone know the name of the bee that lays all of the eggs?" [Queen bee.]

4. Walk the paper queen bee out of the hive. Ask, "What bee is this?" [Queen bee.]

5. Compare her with the demonstration bee. Ask, "Why do you think she is so much larger than the other bees?" (Children often say, "Because she lays all the eggs.") Explain that in order to grow big enough to lay the eggs, the young queen is fed a special food called *royal jelly*.

6. Show "The Queen Bee and Her Eggs" poster. Notice the queen's huge abdomen and the eggs.

New Words:

queen bee
nurse bee
larva, larvae (LAR-vee)
pupa (PEW-pah), pupae (PEW-pee)
cocoon
royal jelly
bee bread
metamorphosis (MET-ah-MORE-fo-siss)

Baby Bees and Nurse Bees

1. Tell the children that when baby bees hatch out of the eggs, they are small, white, worm-like animals called *larvae*. One baby bee is called a *larva*. Have your students say the words, larvae (lar-vee) and larva.

2. Show "The Larvae," poster and have a child point out the larvae and the nurse bee. Explain that the nurse bees feed the larvae royal jelly when they first hatch out of the eggs. Ask, "Which larva do you think just hatched out of an egg?" "Which larva do you think is the oldest?"

3. Tell the children that the older larvae eat a special food called *bee bread*.

4. Say, "Let's find out how bees make bee bread."

   a. Hold up the tray with the cups. Ask the children to pretend with you that the paper cups are cells in the honeycomb. Show the children the cup of honey.

   b. Remind the children that bees carry pollen home in their pollen baskets. Ask, "Where do you think bees hide the pollen?" [In the cells.] Show the children the pretend pollen (graham cracker crumbs) hidden in the paper cup cell.

   c. Take a small amount of pretend pollen out of one cell (cup) and mix it with the honey in another cell (cup).

   d. Tell the children that honey mixed with pollen is called bee bread. Nurse bees feed bee bread to the baby bees.

5. Role-play baby bees and nurse bees.

   a. Give a straw and a cup with honey to every other child. These children are the nurse bees.

   b. Sprinkle pollen into the cups for the children to mix with honey.

Real nurse bees have no direct contact with the larvae. They place food into the cells for the larvae to eat. Step 5 is not totally realistic but expresses the concept that nurse bees feed larvae.

c. Instruct the nurse bees to feed the baby bee (child) who is next to him or her with the straw. (The straw is used as a spoon since the bee bread sticks to the bottom of the straw.)

d. After the baby bees are fed, have the nurse bees throw away their cups and straws. Then have the children reverse roles.

e. Pass out straws and cups with honey to the new nurse bees and repeat the activity.

Change to Adult Bee

1. Tell the children that the larvae eat so much and grow so fast that they soon fill up the cells. Then something exciting happens.

2. Show your students "The Pupae" poster.

a. Have the children notice how dark the cells are. Tell them that the worker bees have covered the cells with wax.

b. Point out the cocoon. Explain that the larvae have made *cocoons* and changed into *pupae* (pew-pee) inside the cocoons. The poster shows what is happening inside the cocoons.

c. Have your students compare changes that they see, observe the legs, wings and body sections, and notice whether or not the pupae have proboscises and antennae. The children will realize that the pupae are turning into adult bees.

d. If appropriate, tell your class that this change from egg to larva to pupa to adult bee is called *metamorphosis*.

3. Place "The Larvae" and "The Pupae" posters side by side, and have your students observe and compare the larvae and pupae.

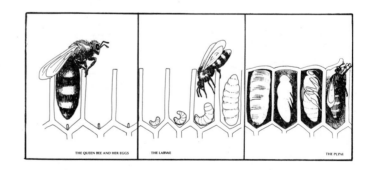

Combine these three posters to show the whole process of bee metamorphosis.

Teacher Demonstration

1. Gather the children in a circle around the large paper hive, and have them think of all the interesting things that are hidden in the tiny wax cells inside a real beehive. Explain that they are going to fill the cells in their hive. Ask, "What could we put in the cells?" [Eggs, baby bees.]

2. Cut the white paper into quarters. Draw an egg, a larva, and a pupa, each on a separate piece of white paper, and glue the paper in the egg carton cells.

3. Ask, "What else is kept in cells in a hive?" [Honey, pollen.] Pretend the brown paper is honey and the yellow is pollen. Cut both the brown and yellow paper into quarters, and paste one piece of each color in separate cells. To make bee bread, paste both yellow and brown pieces in one cell.

Children Fill Their Egg Carton Cells

1. Instruct the children to collect their egg cartons and fill the cells with paper honey, pollen, bee bread, eggs, larvae, and pupae.

2. As the children finish, have them place their egg carton cells inside the large hive.

Going Further

Compare the four stages in the development of the bee (egg, larva, pupa, and adult) to the similar stages that butterflies, moths and many other insects go through. Buy mealworms from a pet shop. Your students can observe the changes from larva (mealworm) to pupa to adult (grain beetle).

Session 3: Young Bees Drama

What You Need

- [ ] mural with flowers
- [ ] paper hive with egg carton cells
- [ ] all the paper bees, including the queen

The cells do not have to be filled in this order. Begin with whichever step the students suggest.

Getting Ready

1. Put the mural with flowers in a convenient place for your students to reach.

2. Place the paper hive in the middle of the circle in the discussion area.

3. Place the queen bee and several paper bees in the hive. Have the remaining bees near your place in the circle.

4. Reread "Young Adult Bees" on page 93 and "Bee Jobs" on page 94.

Young Bees Drama

1. Have the children pretend they are sleepy adult bees that have just chewed their way out of their cells. Encourage them to walk lazily over to the circle and sit down quietly in the discussion area. Ask, "What do you think the sleepy young bees do after they chew their way out of their cells?" Allow time for the children to share their ideas.

2. Expose the inside of the hive, showing the sleepy paper bees and the queen.

3. Dramatize bee behavior, using the children's bees, the queen, and the hive, as you describe the various stages in the development of a young adult bee. The stages listed below are visual or are ones that the children have experienced.

- Keeping eggs warm in their cells. (Have paper bees huddled together on top of egg carton cells.)

- Feeding bee bread to larvae. (Poke nurse bee's head into a larva cell.)

- Taking care of the queen, cleaning her, and feeding her royal jelly. (Have the queen surrounded by a circle of young bees.)

- Producing wax for building cells. (Arrange the bees in lines—chains—and turn them upside down, exposing their wax scales.)

- Fanning their wings to cool the hive.

The activities or jobs that bees do are dependent on their stage of development, and on hive needs. The stages are listed in order under the "Background For Teachers" section on page 94.

4. Explain that when bees are young they work inside the hive because they are not strong enough to fly very far. Older bees fly out to the flowers to gather nectar and pollen.

5. While you distribute the bees, let the children decide whether they want their bees to be young or old.

6. Have the students who chose older bees:

    a. fly their bees to the mural.

    b. pretend the bees are collecting nectar and pollen.

    c. leave their bees on the flowers.

    d. come back to the circle.

7. Encourage the children who chose young bees to:

    a. decide which jobs they want their bees to do inside the hive.

    b. take turns telling the class the job his/her bee does and arranging the young bee on the comb doing its job.

Going Further

Second and third grade students may enjoy writing and illustrating short stories and poems about life inside a honeybee hive or a bee's adventures while collecting nectar and pollen.

If you roll the mural for storage, stack the young bees in one pile and the older bees in another to help you remember which bees are young and which are old.

Optional Activity for a Learning Center

What You Need

For a group of 32, including yourself:

- ☐ 3 bee frames containing brood chambers, honey, and pollen (from a beekeeper)
- ☐ 1 bunch of flowers full of pollen
- ☐ newspaper

For each child and yourself:

- ☐ 1 damp paper towel
- ☐ 1 toothpick

Getting Ready

For each group of five or six children, spread one bee frame on a table on plenty of newspaper. Have real flowers with pollen, damp paper towels, and toothpicks at this table.

Exploring the Bee Frames

Direct the children to the table with the bee frame. Allow plenty of time for your students to open up the cells with toothpicks, examine bee larvae and pupae, and see and feel the difference between the pollen in the cells and the pollen on the flowers. (The pollen in the cells is mixed with a small amount of honey.)

THE QUEEN BEE AND HER EGGS

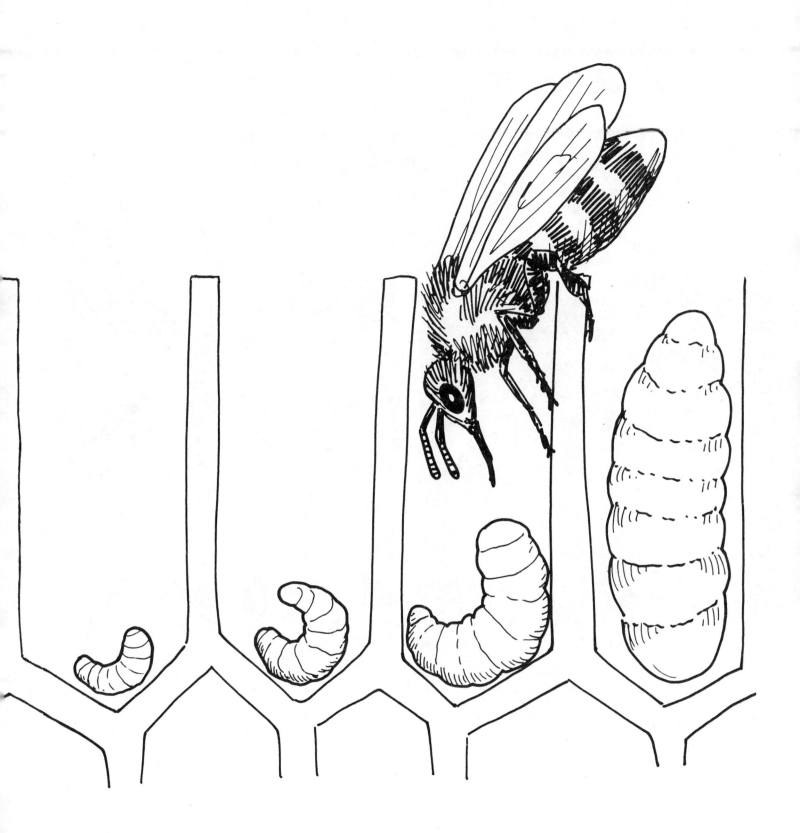

THE LARVAE

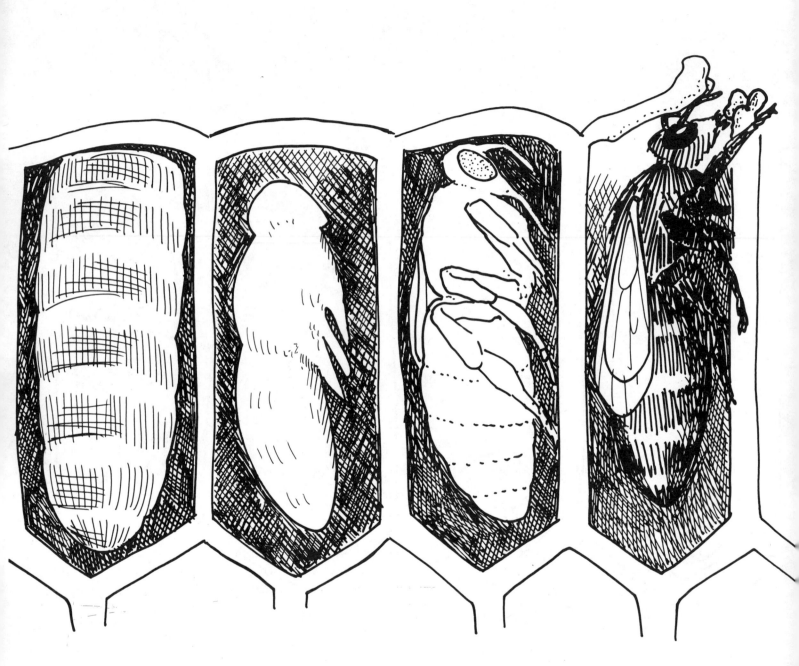

THE PUPAE

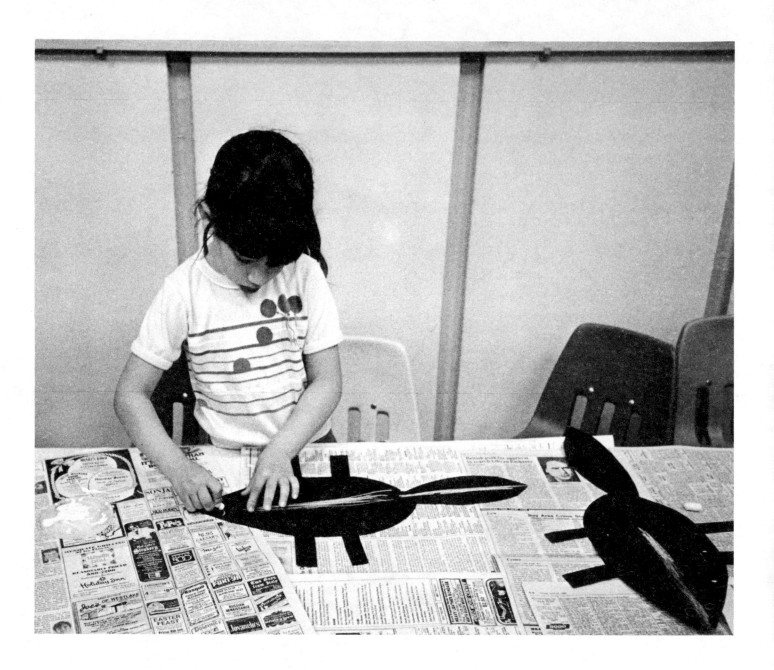

Lesson 5: Bee Enemies

Overview

In this lesson, the students become familiar with bee predators and honey robbers by listening to and discussing the *Bee Enemies* story, and by making a paper skunk. Students role-play guard bees to learn how bees work together to protect the hive.

Time Frame

Bee Enemies	10 minutes
Teacher Demonstration	10 minutes
Children Make Paper Skunks	10 minutes
Role-Playing Guard Bees	20 minutes
Protection	10 minutes

What You Need

For a group of 32, including yourself:

- [ ] mural with bees, flowers, and hive
- [ ] peppermint extract or any familiar scent
- [ ] newspaper
- [ ] white glue or paste
- [ ] 1 plastic bag for cotton balls
- [ ] 1 demonstration tray
- [ ] *Bee Enemies* story, page 57

For each child and yourself:

- [ ] 1 white crayon or piece of chalk
- [ ] 1 pair of scissors
- [ ] 1 sheet of 9" x 12" black construction paper
- [ ] 1 cotton ball

Optional:

- [ ] a different familiar scent
- [ ] extra cotton balls
- [ ] 1 plastic bag for cotton balls

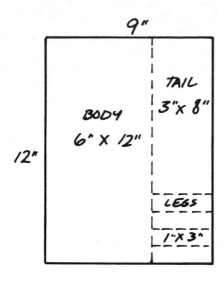

9"

12"

BODY
6" X 12"

TAIL
3"x 8"

LEGS

1"X 3"

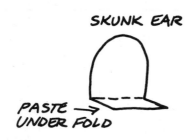

SKUNK EAR

PASTE →
UNDER FOLD

PAPER
SKUNK

Getting Ready

1. Cut construction paper for the skunk predator (see drawings). You and each child will need one sheet of 9" x 12" black construction paper to cut into the following sizes:

- 1 piece 6" x 12" (body with head and ears)

- 1 piece 3" x 8" (tail)

- 4 pieces 1" x 3" (4 legs)

2. Dilute four teaspoons of scent with four table-spoons of water. Pour scent over cotton balls. Squeeze excess liquid out of cotton balls. Put them in a plastic bag.

Optional: Use an additional scent and follow the directions in #2 above, for a later optional activity.

Setting Up The Room

The Work Area

1. Spread newspaper on the tables.

2. Place paste, a white crayon, scissors, and paper for a skunk body, legs, and tail at each child's place.

The Discussion Area

Place in the discussion area:

1. Demonstration tray. Place on a tray: newspaper, paste, a white crayon, scissors, and paper skunk pieces.

2. Scented cotton balls.

3. *Bee Enemies* story, on page 57.

The Mural

If possible, have the mural and the hive near the discussion area. See "Putting the Mural Up," page 71.

Bee Enemies

New Words:

predator
scent

1. Read the short text below out loud to your class, or make up a similar story of your own about bee predators and honey robbers.

Inside a busy beehive, the queen bee is laying eggs and all the other bees are hard at work. Near the hive doorway, some bees are standing guard. The guard bees have to be very watchful, because there are many animals that hurt bees or try to gobble up their honey. Some animals eat bees, like dragonflies, toads, garden spiders, and some birds. Bears, mice, and ants eat the honey that bees make. Dogs and cats play with bees, sometimes killing them. Skunks, who eat both bees and honey, scratch on the outside of the hive to disturb the bees, then catch the bees when they fly out. If you were a guard bee and you saw a toad, or a bear, or a skunk coming up to the hive, what would you do? [Sting.] Sting is exactly what guard bees do when they see a bee enemy coming too close to the hive. That way, all the other bees can continue their work in peace and the queen bee can keep on laying her eggs.

2. Introduce the word *predator*. Explain that an animal that kills other animals for food is called a predator. Have the children name a few bee predators. Reread the story if necessary.

Bears, mice, and ants may also eat bee larvae and pupae, but they are more attracted to the honey.

Teacher Demonstration

1. Ask the children, "What does a skunk eat?" [Both bees and honey.] Let the children share what else they know about skunks.

2. Show the students how to make a paper skunk.

   a. Cut the corners off a 6" x 12" rectangle to make a body and off a 3" x 8" rectangle to make a tail. Save the scraps for ears.

   b. Glue a tail and four leg pieces to the body.

   c. Cut ears out of the paper scraps.

   d. Fold ears at bottom. Apply glue to fold. Place on skunk's head.

e. Draw eyes and a stripe on the skunk, and write your name with chalk or a white crayon on the underside of the skunk.

f. Fold the skunk's legs at the body to make it stand up.

Children Make Paper Skunks

1. Direct the children to the tables to make their skunks.

2. Tell the students to write their names on the undersides of the paper skunks.

Role-Playing Guard Bees

1. Gather the children in the discussion area. Walk a paper skunk over to the hive. Ask, "What do you think would happen if a skunk wandered over to a beehive?" Allow time for the children to share their ideas.

2. Tell the children that the guard bees stay around the hive doorway. They are the middle-aged bees—not too young and not too old. They are the strongest in the bee community. If enemies come near the hive, the guard bees attack. If the guard bees need help, other bees will stop their work and join them. Ask, "How would the bees attack an enemy?" [Sting it.] Explain that one way bees know that an animal is an enemy is by its scent, its smell. Ask, "What do bees have to help them smell an enemy?" [Antennae.]

3. Give each child a scented cottonball. Tell the students that each hive and its bees have their own smell. Have the children pretend they are in a hive. Ask them if they recognize the smell of their hive.

4. Choose several students to be guard bees. Have the rest of the class leave the room. Guard bees stand in a doorway. As the children approach the doorway, the guard bees check them for the hive scent before letting them come back in.

5. Ask, "What do you think would happen if a bee from another hive tried to enter?" [The guard bees would attack because they wouldn't recognize the scent.]

Optional: To vary the activity, secretly select several children to be bees from another hive. Give them cotton balls with a scent that is different from the hive scent. Have these students mix with the rest of the class. If the guard bees detect the strange scent, they prevent the unfamiliar bees from entering the hive.

Protection

1. Discuss with the class some of the ways people are protected.

People need protection from:	Ways people are protected:
cold weather	warm clothes
rain	rain coats
hot weather	cool water

Second and third grade classes may want to make lists.

2. Relate human protection from cold and rainy weather to bees by asking, "How do you think bees are protected from rain and cold weather?" [They stay in the hive. They also cluster to stay warm.]

3. Have the class snuggle together to feel how warm they get.

4. Tell the children that to cool the hive during very hot weather, young bees fan their wings.

5. Have the children fan themselves and each other with their hands to cool off.

Going Further

1. Have the children bring pictures of bee enemies from home. Organize the pictures in 3 groups:

- bee predators (dragonflies, toads, garden spiders, some birds)

- honey robbers (bears, mice, ants)

- bee and honey eaters (skunks)

2. You may want to have a bee party to share the completed mural and some of the activities the children have enjoyed with parents and friends.

Lesson 6: Bee School, Beelines, and Bee Dances

Overview

Students add pollen baskets to their paper bees and learn that pollen gathering is the work performed by older bees. The students role-play going to bee school, flying in a beeline, and communicating messages by doing the round and waggle dances. Pick a sunny day for these outside activities, especially the "bee school."

Time Frame

Bee's Age	5 minutes
Paper Pollen	10 minutes
Bee School	10 minutes
Beelines	5 minutes
Bee Dances	20 minutes
Communicating	10 minutes

What You Need

For a group of 32, including yourself:

- [ ] 9" x 6" piece of yellow construction paper for pollen
- [ ] white glue or paste
- [ ] demonstration bee
- [ ] 1 bunch of real flowers
- [ ] 1 demonstration tray
- [ ] newspaper
- [ ] mural with bees, flowers, beehive, and skunk
- [ ] "Bee Covered with Pollen" poster (master included, page 22)
- [ ] "Bee's Pollen Baskets" poster (master included, page 23)
- [ ] 1 piece of chalk (optional)

Getting Ready

1. Find a place near your school that would be suitable for the role-playing activities. A paved area near a grassy area is ideal, but either will work, as long as there is a nearby building.

2. Place the bunch of real flowers approximately 60 feet from the building. This bunch represents flowers that are near the hive.

3. Cut the yellow paper into 1" x ½" pieces. You and each child will need two pieces.

4. Place newspaper, paste, and paper pollen on the tables.

5. In the discussion area, place a demonstration tray with newspaper, paste, the demonstration bee, and two pieces of paper pollen.

6. Have the "Bee Covered with Pollen" and "Bee with Pollen Baskets" posters near the discussion area.

7. Reread "Bee School," "Bee Communication," "Bee Dances," and "Beeline" on pages 95–96.

The Mural

Place the young bees in the hive and the older bees on or near the flowers. (The students will collect them during class for the activity, "Paper Pollen.")

Bee's Age

1. Gather the children in the discussion area. Tell them that when you watch bees very carefully without disturbing them, you can tell a bee's age by the job it is doing. Ask, "Who remembers some of the jobs that young bees do inside the hive?" [Make wax. Feed the baby bees.]

2. Ask if anyone remembers the job that the middle-age bees do near the hive entrance. [Guard the hive.]

3. Explain that when a bee grows older its wings get stronger and it can fly longer distances. Ask, "What job do you think these bees do?" [Gather nectar and pollen.]

Paper Pollen

1. As a review, show your students the "Bee Covered with Pollen" and "Bee's Pollen Baskets" posters.

2. Tell the class that all of the paper bees are now old enough to fly out to the flowers to collect nectar and pollen.

3. Demonstrate gluing a piece of yellow paper pollen to each of the demonstration bee's back legs.

4. Have the children collect their bees, and go to their work places to glue paper pollen to their bees' back legs.

5. Have the children fly their bees to their paper flowers and pretend the bees are collecting pollen.

Bee School

1. Tell the children that before the bees can go out to gather nectar and pollen, they need to go to "bee school" to learn to find their way back to the hive. Say, "Let's go to our bee school."

2. Go outside. Find a place that would make a good pretend beehive, such as the side of a building.

3. Have the children face the building. Tell them that bee school is held in front of the hive in the morning and again in the afternoon. The bees fly backwards, looking at the hive, so they will remember what the hive and its surroundings look like.

    a. Have the children walk backwards away from the building, stopping several times to note the bushes, trees, walls, and other landmarks that they see at each stop.

    b. Tell the children that bees also use the sun to help them find their way back to the hive.

    c. Ask the students if they feel the sun on their backs, faces, or sides. Have them walk toward the hive, making sure that they still feel the sun where they felt it when they were backing away from the hive.

Beelines

1. Tell the children that when bees go out to gather nectar and pollen, they fly in a straight line called a *beeline*.

You may need to draw a straight line with chalk or find an existing line.

2. Have the students try walking in a straight line. If the children are successful, have them try running in a straight line.

3. Tell the students that bees also fly home in a beeline after they have collected the nectar and pollen.

Bee Dances

Do this activity in groups of 10–12 students, if possible.

1. Ask, "How do you think a bee would tell the other bees about the nectar and pollen?" Let the children share their ideas. Building on your students' responses, explain that bees perform two dances to tell the other bees about the flowers they found.

2. If flowers are nearby, bees do a round dance.

   a. Demonstrate by walking around in a large circle, moving your arms (wings) up and down.

   b. Tell the students that the dancing bee moves her wings rapidly. The wings make a loud, whirring noise. When the other bees hear the noise, they join the dance.

   c. Encourage the children to join you in the round dance.

   d. Mention that as soon as the bees understand the message, they make a beeping sound and fly off to find the flowers. Have the children "fly" to the flowers.

3. Move the bunch of flowers farther away from the building (about 100 feet or more).

4. Explain that bees do a figure-eight dance when flowers are far away. If flowers are very far away, the bees act tired and move very slowly. (Move slowly in a figure-eight, dragging yourself along.) Draw a large figure-eight with chalk (optional).

a. Tell the children that a bee starts the dance by facing in the direction of the flowers. Have the children locate the bunch of flowers. Now face the flowers.

b. Wiggle your hips and move your arms (wings) up and down as you move in the direction of the flowers in the center of the figure-eight. (See drawing.) Tell the children that this dance is also called the waggle dance because bees wiggle their abdomens when they are in the center of the figure-eight. The wiggle sends off more of the flower scent. The smell will help the bees to find the flowers.

c. Complete a figure-eight, wiggling when you are in the center.

d. When the students understand the message, have them make a beeping sound and "fly" off in the direction of the flowers.

5. Move the bunch of flowers. Have a student role-play the dancing bee. Repeat the activity.

6. Hide the flowers. Have one child watch where they are hidden and then communicate the direction of the flowers to the other children by doing the waggle dance.

Starting the dance by facing in the direction of the flowers is a simplification of what really happens in nature. However, the important concept that the bee communicates direction while moving along the center of the figure-eight is made clear.

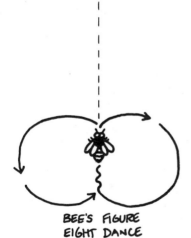

BEE'S FIGURE
EIGHT DANCE

Communicating

1. Review some of the messages bees communicate through their dances. [Scent, direction, and distance of flowers.]

2. Discuss the different ways people communicate nonverbally. Ask questions that stimulate ideas, for example:

- What does a policeman do when he wants you to stop your car? [Raises hand.]

- What do your parents sometimes do when they want you to quiet down? [Put finger in front of mouth.]

- What does it mean when someone shakes his/her head back and forth? [No.] Up and down? [Yes.]

3. Suggest that the children notice different ways people talk with each other, using their hands, heads, faces, and other parts of their bodies.

Going Further

Hide a Butterfly (Preschool–K, with modifications for 1–3)

In *Hide a Butterfly* you use the *Buzzing a Hive* mural of flowers to investigate the relationship between butterflies and flowers. The students learn that butterflies also sip nectar, but with very differently shaped tongues. Children construct paper butterflies and paper bag birds. They camouflage their butterflies on the flowers, and enact the drama of birds trying to find hidden butterflies in a meadow of paper flowers.

Behind the Scenes

Where Do You Find Honeycomb, Pollen, and Dead Bees?

You can do the activities in *Buzzing a Hive* without dead bees, empty honeycomb, and bee frames, but the learning experience is greatly enhanced if you take time to gather these materials. Try to collect them several days before beginning this unit.

Most cities have Bee Associations, which are helpful in supplying materials and valuable information to schools. Beekeepers' supply stores may also provide materials and names of local beekeepers. Look in the yellow pages of your telephone directory under Beekeepers' Supplies.

Local beekeepers are usually quite generous. They may help you obtain empty honeycomb and bee frames with honey and pollen. Sometimes brood frames with bee eggs, larvae, and pupae are available, especially after an unexpected cold spell. Dead bees can be found in large numbers on the ground near beehives. Call a local university or 4-H club to find out if there is an apiary (a place where bees are kept) near you. The beekeeper will probably give you permission to collect dead bees from around the hives.

The following materials are necessary for some of the activities and are available at most health food stores. For 32 people you will need:

- 1 8-oz. package of honey in the comb

- 1 8-oz. jar of honey

Optional materials include:

- dead bees

- bee frames with honey, pollen, bee eggs, larvae, and pupae

- several empty pieces of honeycomb

Caution: Bee Stings!

If you plan to take your class near live bees, contact local health authorities and ask about emergency procedures in case a child is allergic to bee stings. Inquire about a bee sting kit. Also, ask your students' parents if their children have bee allergies, and what they would recommend doing in an emergency.

If a child is stung by a bee, and does not have an allergic reaction to the sting, you can suggest one of several home remedies that may help your student to feel better. Ice or mud packed on the sting is a popular treatment. A paste made from a teaspoonful of baking soda and a few drops of water applied to the sting may bring more relief.

Posters

Eleven 8½" x 11" posters are included in this unit. Larger posters (11" x 14") enhance the quality of the lessons by making it easier for your students to see the drawings from a distance. You can enlarge posters at most photocopying shops for a reasonable price, and some shops give discounts to teachers.

You may also want to use a yellow watercolor marker to highlight the pollen in the "Bee Covered with Pollen" and "Bee's Pollen Baskets" posters. In the "Bee's Pollen Baskets" poster, the pollen is on the center section of the leg in the lower drawing. The yellow coloring will make the pollen easier to recognize and the posters more attractive.

The Mural

A large mural near the discussion area contributes to the quality of the *Buzzing a Hive* unit. However, if mural paper or adequate space are unavailable, your class will still enjoy the activities. You can place the flowers and bees directly on the walls, tables, desks, or floor, or have your students take turns putting their bees and flowers on a smaller mural. Another solution to space constraints is to place the mural in the hallway.

If you do have a mural, make sure that paper bees, flowers, and bee predators can be easily removed from it. The children will want to take their projects home at the end of the *Buzzing a Hive* unit.

- If possible, lay the mural flat on the floor or on a table until after "What's in a Hive?"

- Tape the flowers and grass to the mural. Roll the tape with the sticky side out, and place it between the mural and the flowers or grass so the tape will not show.

- Lay the paper bees on the mural so the children can remove them easily for some of the activities.

- The mural can be rolled up easily for storage.

Putting the Mural Up

After the "What's in a Hive?" lesson, you may decide to hang the mural. If space is available, display the mural on a wall in the classroom near the discussion area. If possible, tack the mural onto a bulletin board so that you can pin the bees on the mural for easy removal. If there is no bulletin board on the walls in your classroom, tape the mural to the wall.

Tape, tack, or glue the hive to the mural. Tape or tack the egg carton cells inside the hive. Pin the queen bee and young bees on the cells. Tape or tack the older bees on the flowers or on the blue sky above the flowers.

Taking the Mural Down

If you plan to have your students take their bees, flowers, egg carton cells, and skunks home immediately after Lesson 6, take the mural down before class and lay it flat on the floor or on a table with the bees, flowers with grass, and hive placed loosely on it. If you plan to do *Hide a Butterfly* next, ask your students to leave their flowers on the mural for the butterflies to visit.

Modifications for Preschool and Kindergarten

While the concepts presented in *Buzzing a Hive* are appropriate for preschool through third grade, activities for such a wide age range require careful modification. For younger children, plan more drama and less discussion. Emphasize activities that children can experience: tasting, seeing, feeling, and role-playing. Keep the activities shorter and use more repetition. Introduce fewer concepts in each lesson. Also, use fewer facts and big words. For example, preschool children can understand the concept of metamorphosis without knowing all the details or the word.

For students who are unskilled with scissors, precut the paper parts for the bees, flowers, hive, and skunk. If you precut the projects, the time frame for the children making the projects will be much shorter than the times listed at the beginning of each lesson. Many of the other activities may also take less time because of the shorter attention span of young children.

Most of the activities in *Buzzing a Hive* are appropriate for preschool and kindergarten. However, suggestions for modifying specific parts of the lessons can be found on the following pages.

Lesson 1: The Honeybee

Making Honeybees in Preschool

1. For preschool children, precut bee bodies out of yellow construction paper using the pattern below.

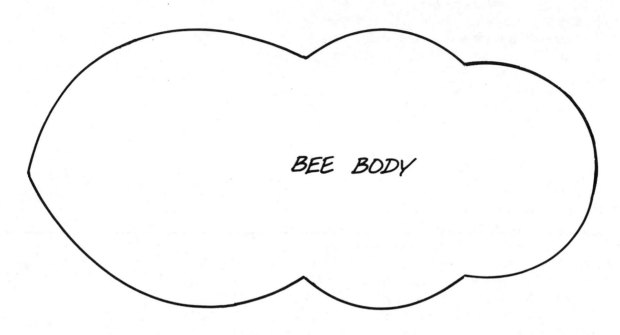

BEE BODY

2. Each bee will need four wings. Precut the wings out of white construction paper using the pattern below.

WINGS

1½"

4½"

3. Cut six legs, one stinger, and two antennae out of black construction paper, using the patterns below:

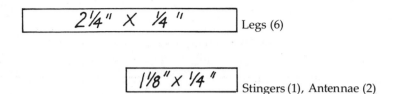

4. During class, the children will observe the bee drawings and you will demonstrate how to make a paper bee. Each child will find the bee's head (the smallest body section) and draw five eyes on the head. Then each child will glue six legs, two antennae, one stinger, and four wings onto his or her bee.

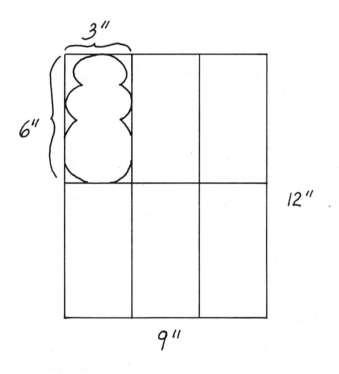

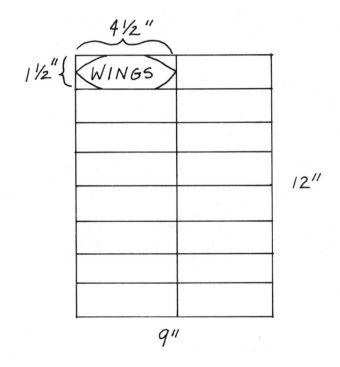

Helpful Hint

When you are precutting the bee bodies and wings, first cut the 9" x 12" construction paper into rectangles. Then stack four rectangles and cut four bodies or four wings at one time.

Making Honeybees in Kindergarten

For kindergarten children who do not use scissors, precut the bee body sections as illustrated below.

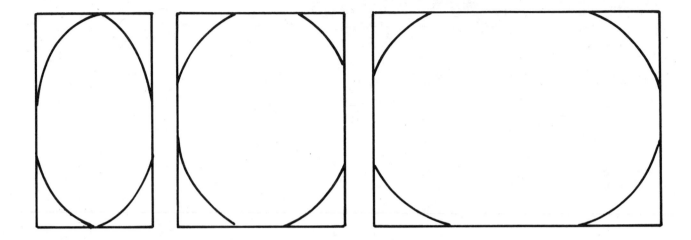

If your students are learning to use scissors, encourage them to cut the corners off the rectangles to make body sections. You may want to precut the wings for kindergarten children as illustrated on page 74. Patterns for the legs, antennae, and stingers are on page 75.

Appropriate New Words

In this lesson, emphasizing the number of body parts a bee has is more important than introducing new words. Therefore, using the words *thorax* and *abdomen* is not recommended for preschool and some kindergarten classes, unless the children are already familiar with these words. You can refer to the three body sections as the smallest (head), middle-size, and largest. Kindergarten students can look at the bee drawings and arrange the paper body sections from smallest to largest, glue them together, and then add the legs, wings, stingers, eyes, and antennae.

You may decide to introduce only the word *antennae*. When the children are ready to glue the antennae onto their bees' heads, have them ask for "antennae" (an-TEN-nee) before you pass the paper antennae to them. New vocabulary words are reinforced when your students have a reason to use them and when they hear their classmates say them. However, if you think the word *antennae* is not appropriate for your age group, use the word *feelers* instead. Also, have the children ask for stingers and then point to the place on their bees where the stinger should be glued.

Writing Names

If your students have difficulty writing their names in small areas, write their names on the paper bees' heads before the class begins. During class, have the children put the paper bee heads (bodies for preschool children) name-side-down on the table ("hide the name"), and then begin gluing the other parts onto the bee.

Step-by-Step

Young children concentrate best when they do an activity one step at a time. When your students are ready to glue the legs, wings, antennae, and stingers onto their bees, first have them count out six paper legs and glue them on the bee. Then have them count out four wings. (When you are setting up the room for this lesson, spread out the legs on a table or counter near the area where the children will be working. Refer to the photograph on this page. Set aside the paper wings to spread out after your students have collected the legs.) By setting out the paper legs and wings at different times, children will focus more easily on the number they need. They can refer to the drawings if they have trouble remembering how many legs or wings the bee has. Also, when you are getting ready for this lesson, set aside the antennae and stingers to pass out as the children ask for them.

Lesson 2: Bees and Flowers, Pollen and Nectar

Making Flowers and Grass in Preschool and Kindergarten

Precut one set of paper flower parts (blossoms, pollen, stems, and leaves) and a rectangle of grass for each student and one set for yourself. The children will glue the grass and flower parts together as a class activity. (Refer to page 19.)

1. Use the orange and white 9" x 12" construction paper to make:

Blossoms:

   a. Design a flower blossom that is at least 9" x 9" or copy the pattern on this page.

   b. Cut out the pattern and place it on top of four sheets of construction paper.

   c. Paper clip the pattern to the paper and cut out the flowers four at a time. (It is not necessary to draw around the pattern.)

Do not cut stamens for preschool and kindergarten students. They will glue the pollen directly to the flower blossoms. Have your students ask for pollen when they are ready to glue the pollen pieces to their flowers.

2. Use the green 9" x 12" construction paper to make:

Stems: Cut out 12" x 1½" rectangles.

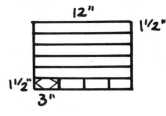

Cut the corners off the rectangles for children who have difficulty using scissors.

←—LEAF—→

Leaves: Cut out 3" x 1½" rectangles.

Grass: Cut out 9" x 4" rectangles.

3. Use the yellow construction paper to make:

Pollen: Cut out 1" x ½" rectangles. Each child will need about four pieces of pollen.

Appropriate New Words

Most young children get pollen and nectar confused. They know that the bee takes something from the flower to make honey, but often have trouble remembering whether it is pollen or nectar. Therefore, it is best to introduce pollen and nectar on separate days, and reinforce their meanings whenever possible. Using the word *stamen* is not recommended, especially if the words *pollen* and *nectar* are new to the children. Many preschool and kindergarten children enjoy using the word *proboscis*. However, use the word *tongue* if you think *proboscis* is too difficult for your students.

More Drama

In Session 2, after the children have sipped pretend nectar with their straw proboscises, have them "fly" out into the school yard and "feel" the nectar turning into honey in their pretend honey stomachs.

The waxed paper scales will eventually peel off of the paper bees, which makes the activity even more realistic. Tell your students that their bees no longer need wax scales because as bees get older, they stop making wax for the hive and begin new jobs.

Lesson 3: Building a Beehive

Adding Wax Scales

Cut the waxed paper into ½" x ½" squares for wax scales. You and each child will need at least four wax scales to glue directly onto the bee's abdomen and at least four more to glue onto the egg carton cells. You will not need to cut the 1½" x 2½" yellow rectangles since your students will not use slits to hold the scales on their bees. (Compare the drawing on page 30 with the drawing on this page.)

Making a Large Beehive

Cut the lids off the egg cartons, write your students' names on the cartons, and cut out the large hive following the instructions on page 28. Your students will be able to do all of the other activities in this lesson.

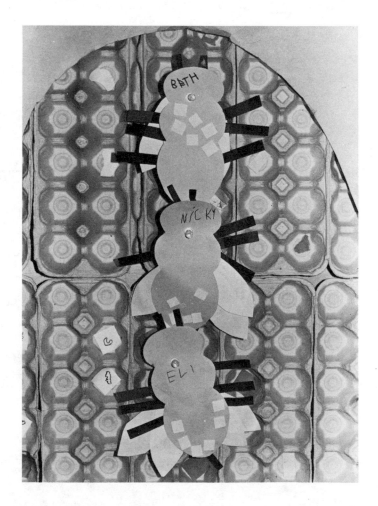

Making Paper-bag Hives (Optional)

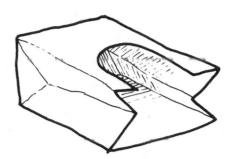

At the end of the *Buzzing a Hive* unit, preschool and kindergarten children may enjoy making their own paper-bag hives. Paper bees, flowers, and skunks will fit neatly inside the paper-bag hives for the children to take home. Many of the concepts introduced in this unit will be reinforced when the children play with their creations at home.

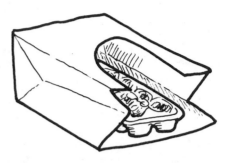

To prepare a paper bag hive, cut a 3″ strip off the top of the bag so that the hive will stand up. Cut an arched doorway in each hive.

Your students will fill their egg carton cells during Lesson 4. Then at the end of this unit, they can glue their egg cartons into the precut paper-bag hives.

Lesson 4: What's in a Hive?

Appropriate New Words

The changes that occur during metamorphosis fascinate young children. Most kindergarten and many preschool children know that caterpillars turn into butterflies or moths. Learning that bees hatch from eggs and go through several changes before emerging from their cells as adult bees is a concept that young children can understand, if presented carefully. Use fewer new words. For example, it is not necessary to use the word *metamorphosis.* Understanding the changes that occur is important, not the word itself.

Kindergarten students can learn and understand the words *larvae* and *pupae.* Using these words with preschool children depends on how much time you are willing to spend introducing and reinforcing new vocabulary. Since the children are exposed to so many new ideas in this lesson, you can simplify "What's in a Hive?" by referring to larvae and pupae as baby bees.

Royal jelly, food for the queen and the newly-hatched larvae, is interesting, but it provides one more new word and concept in a lesson that already has too much content for preschool or kindergarten children to absorb in one day. Be selective and decide ahead of time which concepts to emphasize, introduce in a later session, or eliminate. You can delete royal jelly and concentrate on beebread and metamorphosis; or you can emphasize bee foods, and spend a whole lesson on royal jelly and beebread.

If you decide to spend a whole lesson on bee foods, have the newly-hatched larvae (children) eat royal jelly (vanilla pudding or custard) and pretend they are growing older. Then have them eat beebread (graham cracker crumbs and honey). Place the emphasis on eating and growing so big that the baby bee fills the whole cell. On another day, concentrate on the baby bee building a cocoon, the changes inside the cocoon, and the emergence of the young adult bee.

More Role-Playing

After you finish the activity "Change to Adult Bee," encourage the children to act out the growth process from egg to adult bee by:

1. Curling up on the floor (egg).

2. Pretending to eat, and slowly standing up and stretching (larva eating and growing bigger).

3. Standing with eyes closed (pupa in cocoon).

4. Chewing their way out of an imaginary cell.

5. Emerging as a sleepy adult bee.

Filling Egg Carton Cells

Before class begins, cut the yellow, brown, and white construction paper into 1" squares. You and each child will need four squares of each color. The children will enjoy gluing the yellow paper pollen and the brown paper honey into their egg carton cells. For preschool children, you may want to pre-cut the white paper into egg shapes or have the children draw only eggs to glue into their cells. Most preschool children would have a difficult time drawing baby bees on such small pieces of paper. However, most kindergarten children get very involved in drawing eggs, larvae, and pupae.

More Drama

Even though there is so much drama in this lesson, you can still add more, especially during the teacher demonstration and the "Children Fill Their Egg Carton Cells" activity. Before the class begins, sprinkle the yellow paper pollen in the center of the paper flowers that are lying on the mural, which is on the floor. During the class, before you demonstrate filling the egg carton cells with pollen, go over to the mural. Have a paper bee collect pollen from a flower. Fly the bee back to the children. Ask, "Where do you think bees hide the pollen?" [Cells.] Glue yellow paper pollen in the cells.

Most children want to collect pollen from their own flowers and may turn the flowers over looking for their names. Tell your students that bees visit more than one flower. Their bees can pick up pollen from any of the flowers.

When the children are ready to glue paper pollen into their egg carton cells, encourage them to collect pollen from the paper flowers and glue the pollen into their paper cells.

Also, as the children are filling their cells, walk around with the paper queen bee and pretend she is laying eggs in the children's cells. (A good way to distribute precut paper eggs.) If you decide to have your students draw baby bees, walk around with your demonstration bee, poking her head into the cells and pretending she is feeding the larvae. Visiting the cells with the paper queen or nurse bee is an excellent way to acknowledge the drawings the children have created.

Fewer Choices

In "Young Bees Drama," the number of choices may be overwhelming for preschool children. Offer them fewer choices. Let them choose between pretending that their paper bees are young bees that work in the hive or older bees that leave the hive to collect pollen and nectar. If you want to concentrate only on hive jobs, give the children two choices, such as taking care of the queen or feeding the larvae. Kindergarten children can handle more choices.

Lesson 5: Bee Enemies

Making Paper Skunks

Precut the skunk's body, tail, legs, and ears. The ears can be cut from paper scraps. Then fold the ears at the bottom. (See the drawings on this page.)

During the class, you will demonstrate how to make a skunk and the children will paste the skunk body parts together as a class activity. When you distribute the ears, instruct your students to place the paste under the fold to make the ears stand up on the skunk's head.

More Drama

In this lesson, children learn about animals that attack bees and beehives. You will introduce this idea by reading the *Bee Enemies* story. Use toy animals, preferably realistic looking ones, to dramatize the discussion that follows the *Bee Enemies* story. If you need props for this activity, suggest that the children bring from home: a toy skunk, mouse, bear, dog, cat, toad, bird, dragonfly, spider, or ant. Hide the toy animals in a large paper bag near the hive. After reading the story, bring the animals out one at a time and discuss which of the toy animals eat bees, which eat honey, and which do both. For example, you could walk a toy bear over to the hive, saying, "What do you think the hungry bear is looking for, bees or honey?" Do the same thing with the other animals.

If precutting and folding the skunk ears is too time consuming, have the children draw the ears directly on the skunk with white chalk or crayons.

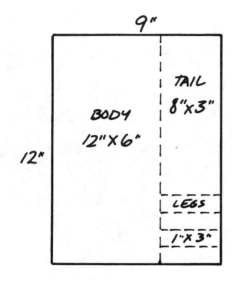

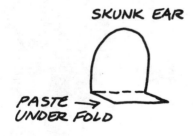

SKUNK EAR

PASTE → UNDER FOLD

PAPER SKUNK

Appropriate New Words

Do not introduce the word *predator* to preschool children. Concentrating on what the different animals eat is enough for this age group. Some kindergarten classes may be ready to learn the word, but understanding the concept is more important.

Lesson 6: Bee School, Beelines, and Bee Dances

Gathering Pollen

Before your class begins, sprinkle paper pollen in the center of the paper flowers. During the "Paper Pollen" activity, tell your class that all of the paper bees are now old enough to fly out to the flowers to collect nectar and pollen. Fly your bee to the mural to collect pollen. Hold the paper pollen onto each of the bee's back legs as you fly the bee back to the demonstration tray. Show your students how to glue a piece of yellow paper pollen to each of the bee's back legs. Have several children at a time find their paper bees and fly them over to the flowers to pick up paper pollen. Have them fly their bees over to the tables to glue pollen to the bees' back legs. They will then fly their bees to the mural and leave them on the flowers.

Fewer Instructions

For preschool and kindergarten, the bee dances need to be simplified. For preschool children, introduce the idea that bees communicate the distance to the flowers by doing two dances, the round dance and the waggle dance. If the flowers are near, bees do the round dance. If they are far away, bees do the waggle dance. The children can do these dances, and verbalize whether the flowers are near or far away. For kindergarten children, introduce the concept of the direction of the flowers while doing the waggle dance (see page 65), but emphasize the idea that bees do the round dance when the flowers are near and the waggle dance when the flowers are far away.

Background for Teachers

This background section is for your information and use, and is not meant to be read out loud to your students. The detailed information is presented to help you answer most of the questions your enthusiastic students will ask. Some of the questions children ask most often are in the margins near related background material.

Information about bees varies depending on the author and the publication date. The following is a synthesis of information researched from many sources.

Bee Society

Honeybees live in a highly organized society that often contains as many as 70,000 members. During late spring and summer, a bee colony consists of three kinds of honeybees: one queen, several hundred drones, and thousands of workers. The queen lays all the eggs and keeps the colony together. The drone bees, the only males in the bee society, fertilize young queens. The worker bees do a variety of jobs in the hive and also gather nectar and pollen from the fields.

A five-year-old boy asked, "Is there a king bee?"

Body Structure of Queens, Drones, and Workers

All honeybees, like other insects, have bodies that are divided into three sections: a head, a thorax, and an abdomen. Bees have six legs, four wings, and five eyes. The two large compound eyes, one on each side of the bee's head, consist of thousands of individual eyes that enable the bee to see in many directions. The three small, simple eyes in a triangle on the top of the bee's head are sensitive to light, telling the bee when to start and stop the day's activity and helping the bee to navigate to and from food sources. The two antennae on the front of the bee's head are slender, jointed feelers used for smelling, touching, and possibly for hearing.

"Does the queen have a stinger?"

Queens, drones, and workers have some body parts that are modified to perform highly specialized tasks. The queen bee has an enlarged abdomen for her job of laying up to 2,000 eggs each day. Drones have huge eyes to help them find young queens during mating flights. Both queens and workers have stingers, but the stingers are designed for different purposes. The queen stings only other queens to defend her position in the hive. She may need to sting many times during her life. Therefore, she has a smooth, curved stinger that is easily removed from the victim without damaging herself. In contrast, the worker dies when its barbed stinger is lodged in the victim's body. The worker bee's purpose in stinging is to protect the colony. The barbs make the bee's defense more effective. The drone bee has no stinger and no need for one, since mating with a queen is the drone's only function.

Bee Sizes

The three kinds of honeybees also vary in size. An egg-laying queen is the largest because of her huge abdomen. Drones are shorter than queens, but have bulkier heads and thoraxes. The worker bee is the smallest of the three, measuring about one-half inch long.

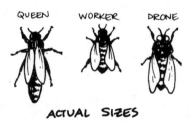

Pollen and Nectar

The worker bee supplies the bee colony with nectar and pollen. Flowers produce nectar, which is a sweet liquid, and pollen, which is high in protein. Honeybees need both for food. The worker bee's body is beautifully adapted for collecting these foods and carrying them back to the hive. Her body hairs pick up pollen as she moves around in flowers. Her hind legs are provided with small rakes and presses for packing pollen into the long, sturdy, hind-leg hairs, called pollen baskets. The mouthpiece of the worker bee forms a long tube-like proboscis for sucking nectar out of flowers. The worker has a special stomach, called a honey sac, crop, or honey stomach, for storing and transporting nectar.

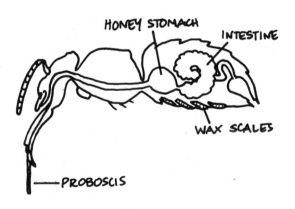

The process of changing nectar into honey begins in the bee's honey sac. Even as the worker is flying to her hive, body chemicals are added to the nectar to break it down into easily digested sugars. At the hive, the forager empties her honey sac onto the mouthparts of younger bees. These bees, by alternately sucking and blowing, roll the nectar on their tongues to evaporate the water. The nectar is then placed in honeycomb cells. Evaporation continues as other bees fan their wings. When the nectar thickens into honey, bees cap the cells with wax for storage.

Colors that Bees See

The colors of flowers play an important part in attracting bees to nectar and pollen. However, a bee's color vision is not like our own. Bees see only four colors: yellow, blue-green, blue, and ultra-violet. According to experiments performed by scientist Karl von Frisch, orange, yellowish-green, and all the yellow shades look yellow to the bee. Bees are unable to see scarlet red, but red flowers with a purple or mauve tint are believed to appear blue. White seems bluish-green to a honeybee.

The flower colors of orange and white chosen for this activity are ones that attract bees. Red was excluded since it is not considered a "bee color." However, bees do visit some red flowers, such as dahlias, because of their purple tints and their large, bright yellow pollen centers.

Beehives

In the wild, a colony of honeybees often makes its home in a dark, protected place such as a hollow tree trunk. Many years ago, people began to construct beehives and raise bees. The early beehive was made out of straw, which was light and easy to move. However, the colony was often destroyed when the honey was removed. At present, the wooden beehive is used in most countries, because its removable parts allow the beekeeper to gather honey while the colony remains intact.

The tree trunk, straw hive, and wooden hive provide only external protection for the colony. Honeybees actually build their own home by producing wax. The wax is made in wax glands inside each worker bee's body. The glands produce flat pieces of wax, called wax scales, which ooze from the bee's bodies as they hang in chains. These workers also remove the scales from the undersides of their abdomens with tiny spurs on their middle legs. They then use their legs, jaws, and bodies to push and shape the wax to form perfect six-sided or hexagon-shaped cells. The many cells form the comb which is divided into honeycomb and brood comb. In the cells of the brood comb, young bees experience a remarkable metamorphosis.

Bee Metamorphosis and Diet

Each day a queen bee lays between 1,200 and 2,000 eggs, some fertilized and some not. The unfertilized eggs hatch into drones and the fertilized eggs into workers or queens.

Since there is only one queen to a hive, eggs that develop into queens are laid only when the queen is growing old or is showing signs of leaving the hive to start a new one. The queen eggs are laid in enlarged cells shaped somewhat like peanuts. When the eggs hatch, white worm-like larvae emerge from the eggs. Worker bees feed the queen larvae a special food called royal jelly or bee's milk, which is a milky substance produced in the bee's head glands. It is believed that the diet of royal jelly gives the queen her large size and incredible egg-laying ability.

The fertilized eggs in the smaller cells of the brood comb develop into worker bees. For the first three days after hatching, the worker bee larvae are fed royal jelly. For the next three days they are fed bee bread, a combination of honey and pollen.

Diet alone seems to determine whether a fertilized bee egg will develop into a queen or a worker. If a queen suddenly dies and no queen larvae exist, a nurse bee can change a newly-hatched worker larva into a queen by feeding it a diet that consists only of royal jelly. However, if the larva is over three days old and has started eating bee bread, the larva will grow into a worker.

Along the edge of a brood comb, bullet-shaped cells are often found. These cells are larger than worker cells and house the developing drones. Drone larvae are fed a special food similar to royal jelly.

When a honeybee larva is fully grown, a worker bee caps the cell with wax. The larva spins a silken cocoon, sheds its skin, and enters its pupal stage. Hidden in its capped cell, the pupa completes its dramatic change to an adult bee. This transformation from egg to adult takes 24 days for a drone, 20 for a worker, and 16 for a queen.

Young Adult Bees

When young adult bees chew their way out of their wax enclosures, they perform different tasks depending on which type they are:

- Queens quickly sting to death all immature queens still in their cells and fight other recently emerged queens. At 7–10 days old, the young queen takes her mating flight, is fertilized, and returns to the hive to lay eggs.

- Drones rest and eat for ten days, and then begin their mating flights to fertilize queens.

- Worker bees begin a series of jobs.

Bee Jobs

The age of the worker and the needs of the bee society determine the order in which workers do their jobs. Listed below are the jobs and the approximate ages of the worker as she performs her tasks during normal summer conditions.

	Job	Age of Worker
1.	Incubates cells by resting on them, cleans cells, and helps younger bees chew out of cells.	0–3 days
2.	Feeds beebread to old larvae.	3–5 days
3.	Produces royal jelly to feed queen and new larvae. Also attends queen, and continues to feed old larvae.	5–12 days
4.	Produces wax to build and repair hive.	12–21 days
5.	Works near hive entrance.	2–3 weeks
	• Fans wings to cool hive and evaporate water from honey.	
	• Receives nectar and pollen to place in cells.	
	• Guards hive.	
6.	Gathers nectar and pollen.	3–6 weeks

Honeybees are extremely flexible, and can change jobs whenever necessary. For example, the growth of a bee's wax-producing glands allows the 12–21 day old bee to build and repair comb, but the same bee can also cool the hive, receive nectar and pollen, or guard the hive.

Hive jobs are usually performed during the first half of the honeybee's life. Honeybees gather food during the last half of their lives.

Bee School

Before going out to the fields to collect nectar and pollen for the first time, bees need to orient themselves to their hive and its immediate surroundings. To learn how the hive looks from the outside, bees hover in front of their home, facing it while slowly flying backwards. Later, they take short excursions, each one longer than the last, using the sun, trees, and different landmarks to help them find their way home.

Bee Communication

Once bees are familiar with the appearance of the hive from a distance, they fly out to the fields to forage. When a scout bee discovers a rich food source, she returns to the hive and excitedly communicates information about the scent, the distance, and the direction of the flowers.

Back at the hive, the scent, which lingers on the scout's body, and the nectar, which the awaiting foragers smell and taste, convey messages about the kind of flowers found. Out in the field, scent left on the flowers by the scout helps the foragers to locate the food source.

"Can bees talk?"

Bee Dances

The scout bee communicates more information about the flowers through dances. If the flowers are within 100 yards of the hive, the scout dances in circles on the honeycomb. The round dance informs the other bees to search near the hive for food.

When the flowers are more than 100 yards from the hive, the scout needs to convey messages about the direction. She does this at the beginning of a figure-eight or waggle dance. If the flowers are in the direction of the sun, the scout moves in a straight line up the surface of the honeycomb, wiggling her abdomen as she goes. When the flowers are in the opposite direction, she moves down the honeycomb. The direction of the flowers either to the right or the left of the sun is also communicated by the dancer. As other bees gather around, the scout continues her dance, repeating the message each time she wiggles along the straight run connecting the loops of the figure-eight.

The speed with which the figure-eight dance is performed also communicates specific information about distance. If the dance is performed rapidly, the nectar is about 100 yards from the hive. The extremely slow movements of an exhausted bee indicate that the food source is as far away as two miles.

The movement of the bee's wings creates a buzzing sound. The degree of loudness indicates distance. If the bee has flown a long distance, she is tired and moves her wings slowly, producing very little sound. Loud buzzing conveys the message that the flowers are nearby.

Beeline

After the dancing bee communicates information about the location of the food source, the bees fly to the flowers in a straight line, commonly known as a beeline. Once there, the bees fly from flower to flower collecting nectar or pollen. Then, heavily laden with food, they take the most direct route home, in a beeline.

Bee's Lifespan

The lifespan of queens, workers, and drones varies greatly. The queen may live up to five years. Drones usually are raised in the late spring and live through one summer. During the busy summer months, workers survive for about six weeks. During the cold weather, they live up to six months since they are relatively inactive.

African Honeybees

In the last few years, African bees have made the news, with the media often emphasizing the aggressive nature of the so-called "killer bees." This sensationalism leaves the public with uneasy feelings about an imminent arrival of these bees in the United States. But what are the "killer bees?" Where did they come from? What are they really like? How do they differ from other bees?

The original honeybee evolved into several species and subspecies as it spread throughout the world. The honeybees of Africa adapted to a warm climate. They built small nests containing little honey, because they did not need to store honey for their winter survival. Since they had no need to build nests inside hollow trees for protection against the cold, their nests were often exposed to predators. In order to fiercely protect these nests, African honeybees developed nervous, defensive temperaments.

The European honeybee adapted to a climate in which the summers are warm and the winters cold. They made nests inside well-insulated hollows to protect themselves against the winter cold, storing large quantities of honey to provide them with food during the winter months. Since their nests were well-hidden from their enemies, European honeybees developed gentle, less defensive temperaments.

Climate still strongly affects the bees that exist today, influencing their temperaments, their honey and beeswax production, and their efficiency in pollinating plants. Although African bees are slightly smaller than European bees and have stings that are no more painful or harmful, once aroused they respond more quickly, sting in much larger numbers with less provocation, and chase enemies farther than European bees. African honeybees are less productive honey and beeswax providers and less efficient plant pollinators.

The honeybees in the United States are of European origin. The African bees spread from Africa to Brazil in the 1950s and then to Mexico. A few colonies were discovered in the United States between 1985 and 1989, but were quickly eradicated. Scientists are working on ways to prevent the African bee from entering the United States. In addition to their concern for people and livestock, scientists fear that the African bee could gradually replace the European bee in the southern states, therefore lowering honey and beeswax production, as well as damaging crops dependent on bee pollination.

Should the African bee enter the United States, scientists are planning ways to control it. One possible solution is breeding it with the European bee to create a gentler, more productive species of African bee.

References

Children's Books

Deutsch, A. *Bees and Honey*. Oxford Scientific Films. New York, G.P. Putnam & Sons, 1977. (Large color photographs, but adult text.)

Goudey, A.E. *Here Come the Bees!* New York, Charles Scribner's Sons, 1960.

Hawes, J. *Bees and Beelines*. New York, Thomas Y. Crowell Co., 1964.

———— *Watch Honeybees With Me*. New York, Thomas Y. Crowell Co., 1964.

Platt, R. *Secrets of Life*. New York, Simon and Schuster, 1957.

Rood, R.N. *Ants and Bees*. New York, Wonder Books, Inc., 1962.

Russell, F. *The Honeybees*. New York, Alfred A. Knopf, 1967.

Simon, H. *Exploring the World of Social Insects*. New York, Vanguard Press, Inc., 1962.

Teale, E.W. *The Bees*. Chicago, Children's Press, Inc., 1967.

Adult Books

Farb, P. *The Insects*. Life Nature Library. New York, Time, Inc., 1962.

Frisch, K. von *The Dancing Bees: An Account of the Life and Senses of the Honeybee*. London: Methuen and Co., Ltd., 1954.

———— *The Dance Language and Orientation of Bees*. Cambridge, Massachusetts, Belknap Press of Harvard University Press, 1967.

Ipsen, D.C. *What Does a Bee See?* Reading, Massachusetts, Addison-Wesley Publishing Co., Inc., 1971. (Grade 5 to adult.)

James, W.R. *Know Your Poisonous Plants*. Healdsburg, California, Naturegraph Publishers, 1973.

Marler, P.R. *Marvels of Animal Behavior*. Washington, D.C., National Geographic Society, 1974.

Study Prints

AEVAC Study Prints—*The Variety of Living Things, Honeybee*. Produced by McGraw-Hill Films in collaboration with The California Academy of Sciences.

Assessment Suggestions

Selected Student Outcomes

1. Students identify structures and behaviors that help the honeybee survive in the wild.

2. Students articulate how and why bees collect pollen and nectar from flowers.

3. Students describe the different jobs that bees perform in their hives during their lifetime and the activities that occur inside the hive.

4. Students identify honey and beeswax as two products that come from bees and are helpful to people today.

5. Students gain knowledge about the life cycle of a bee.

6. Students are able to identify bee predators.

Built-In Assessment Activities

Getting to Know Honeybees
In Lesson 1, The Honeybee, students study a honeybee drawing, share their personal experiences with bees, and may view live bees outdoors or closely examine dead bees. Students also build a paper model of a bee to use in dramas. During these activities, the teacher can look for perceptive student responses such as "Bees have a stinger to protect themselves from enemies," or "My bee has lots of eyes to see all around." The paper models are a tool to assess what students understand about bee structure. (Outcome 1)

Honeybees and Flowers
In Lesson 2, Bees and Flowers, Pollen, and Nectar, students are introduced to the relationship between bees and flowers as they participate in a variety of multi-sensory activities. They observe real flowers, collect real pollen, sip juice for nectar, and taste honey. Next, they use a model flower and bee to enact dramas where bees collect pollen and nectar. The teacher can question the students during the activities, and listen to their thoughts and ideas. Observations of the planned and spontaneous bee dramas can also provide valuable information about what the students have learned. (Outcomes 1, 2)

Bee Jobs

Through activities in Lessons 1–4, students are introduced to the many jobs that bees perform during their lifetime. During Lesson 4, Young Bees Drama, students use their bee and hive models to review bees' jobs and choose a job for their bees. The teacher can listen for detailed descriptions of the various bee jobs and evidence of new vocabulary related to bee life such as bee bread, larva, wax, collecting pollen, nectar, and queen bee. (Outcome 3)

Bees and People

In Lessons 2–4, students learn that bees make honey from nectar and that bees make the wax for their honeycomb. They also see how bees use the hexagon shape to build a strong hive structure. To relate what bees do to their own life experiences, students taste honey, touch items made from beeswax, and collect everyday items built with the hexagon shape. The teacher can lead a discussion about how bee products are used by people or she can challenge students to bring in items from home that contain honey, beeswax, or the hexagon shape. Parents can help their children make a list of such items that they find at the grocery store. (Outcome 4)

Additional Assessment Ideas

Bee Books

Use drawings in the guide and student drawings as the basis for student writing and/or dictation about honeybees. The stories can be fanciful tales mixed with ideas from honeybee life and natural history. (Outcomes 1–6)

Beekeepers and Living Hives

At the end of the unit, invite a beekeeper to talk with your class or visit a living hive at a science center. Listen to the quality and kinds of questions and responses that come from the students. (Outcomes 1–6)

Bee Metamorphosis

Ask students to draw the different phases of a bee's life cycle, from egg to adult bee. (Outcome 5)

Bee Enemies

In Lesson 5, Role-Playing Guard Bees, students learn about bee defenses. Ask students to draw a picture and tell about, "The Day the Honeybee Hive Was Raided." (Outcome 6)

Literature Connections

This GEMS unit guides children through the fascinating world of a **honeybee community**, their **food gathering, life cycle, defenses, and interdependence with flowers**. Most of the books listed involve the **ecology** of the honeybee or how a bee's life is intertwined with other living things. *In the Tall, Tall Grass* and *The Rose in My Garden* use rhyming verse to illustrate the interconnectedness of meadow life with bees as important players. *The Bee Tree* makes a great connection between learning about bees and the joy of reading. Where *Butterflies Grow* describes the butterfly life cycle; a nice comparison to bee **metamorphosis**. And in a classic book, **honey** is central to a story about a familiar bear and his encounter with bees.

The Bee Tree
by Patricia Polacco
Philomel Books, The Putnam & Grosset Group, New York, 1993
Grades: Preschool–4

When Mary Ellen tires of reading, her "Grampa" suggests a search for a bee tree, which soon involves the entire community. Do the "bee dances" and "beeline" flight patterns in the GEMS activities relate to the storybook? This enchanting book is not only a great connection to *Buzzing a Hive*, but also flows very sweetly with strong life lessons: the joy of reading, the special communication possible between old and young, and the awareness, in the words of "Grampa" that "...adventure, knowledge, and wisdom....do not come easily. You have to pursue them. Just like we ran after the bees to find their tree, so you must also chase these things through the pages of a book!" This would also be an excellent book to read in connection with the GEMS/PEACHES guide *Tree Homes*.

The Flower Alphabet Book
by Jerry Pallotta; illustrated by Leslie Evans
Charlesbridge Press, Watertown, Massachusetts 1988
Grades: Preschool–2

Beautiful alphabet picture book showing many varieties of flowers and plants in accurate detail. Would make a good early primary accompaniment to the meadows ideas in *Hide a Butterfly* and the activities relating to nectar, pollen, and flowers in *Buzzing a Hive*.

A House is a House for Me
by Mary Ann Hoberman;
illustrated by Betty Fraser
Viking Penguin, New York. 1978
Grades: K–3

Lists in rhyme the dwellings of various animals, peoples, and things such as a shell for a lobster or a glove for a hand. Nice extension to "Lesson 3: Building A Bee Hive."

In the Tall, Tall Grass
written and illustrated
by Denise Fleming
Henry Holt and Co., New York. 1991
Grades: Preschool–3

Rhyming text and vibrant collage illustrations look at the world of creatures you might see in the long, tall grass. Their behaviors are captured in catchy rhymes as caterpillars lunch, hummingbirds sip and dip, bees strum, ants lug, and moles ritch, ratch and scratch.

Michael Bird-Boy
by Tomie dePaola
Simon & Schuster, New York. 1975
Grades: K–3

A young boy who loves the countryside determines to find the source of the black cloud that hovers above it. When he discovers the source of this pollution, a factory making "genuine" artificial honey syrup, he helps the "boss-lady" set up beehives so she can make natural honey without creating pollution.

Pretend You're A Cat
by Jean Marzollo; illustrated by Jerry Pinkney
Dial Books, New York. 1990
Grades: Preschool–1

Wonderful illustrations and friendly verses ask children to pretend they are different animals and to act out the animal's behavior. "Can you buzz? Are you covered with fuzz?" Great springboard to a discussion of similarity and differences among animal behaviors. Animals include a cat, pig, snake, bear, horse, seal, and bee.

The Rose in My Garden
by Arnold Lobel; illustrated by Anita Lobel
Greenwillow Books, New York. 1984
Grades: Preschool–2

Each page adds a new rhyming line to a poem as a beautiful garden of flowers, insects, and animals grows. A surprise interaction among the garden residents takes place at the end of the book. Young readers will enjoy the repeated patterns in the story.

When I'm Sleepy
by Jane R. Howard; illustrated by Lynne Cherry
E.P. Dutton, New York. 1985
Grades: Preschool–2

> A young girl speculates about sleeping in places other than her bed and is shown sleeping with twelve different animals in a nest, a swamp, standing up, hanging upside down, etc. The witty, glowing illustrations and active verbs capture a wide range of habitats and possibilities.

Where Butterflies Grow
by Joanne Ryder; illustrated by Lynne Cherry
Lodestar Books, New York. 1989
Grades: K–5

> Here's an imaginative description of what it might feel like to grow from a tiny egg into a black swallowtail butterfly. Structure, metamorphosis, locomotion, camouflage, and feeding behaviors are all described from the point of view of the butterfly. There's also a page of gardening tips on how to attract butterflies. Outstanding illustrations include detailed drawings of metamorphosis.

Winnie-The-Pooh
by A.A. Milne; illustrations by Ernest H. Shepard
E.P. Dutton, New York. 1926
Dell Publishing, New York. 1954
Grades: K–5

> This well-loved classic contains chapter after delightful chapter of the adventures of Christopher Robin, Pooh, and their animal friends. Relevant chapters include one in which bees are encountered; several in which logic is applied to solve a problem; and an adventure in navigation.

A teacher wrote to the GEMS Network News, our national newsletter, to suggest two more books that can help start off this unit. The books are The Honeybee and the Robber *by Eric Carle and* The Old Ladies Who Liked Cats *by Carol Greene. Please send us your suggestions, for inclusion in this guide, and in the GEMS literature connections handbook,* Once Upon A GEMS Guide: Connecting Young People's Literature to Math and Science.

Summary Outlines

Lesson 1: The Honeybee

Observations
1. Introduce honeybee, using "The Honeybee" poster, with questions and discussion.
2. Distribute "The Honeybee" posters.
3. Identify 3 main body sections.
4. Locate and discuss antennae.
5. Have students count all parts.
6. Ask questions to encourage observations.

Teacher Demonstration
1. Introduce the mural.
2. Demonstrate making paper bee by having students look at posters, and asking questions about how many of each part a bee has, then cutting out and gluing part(s) on (see instructions and illustrations on pages 10, 11).

Children Make Paper Honeybees
1. Have students cut out, arrange, and glue together paper bee body sections, count out and glue on legs, antennae, and stingers. Count, cut out, and glue on wings.
2. Have students write names on underside of bee's head.
3. Have students place bees in mural "sky."

Reviewing
Bring class together to review number of bee body parts.

Lesson 2: Bees and Flowers, Pollen and Nectar

Session 1: Pollen

Pollen Packers
1. Encourage the children to discuss their observations of real bees on flowers.
2. Distribute flowers with yellow pollen.
3. Pass cotton ball to each child, and have children roll cotton balls in flowers.
4. Ask if they know what the yellow dust is called. [**Pollen.**] Explain that bees eat pollen.
5. Show "Bee Covered with Pollen" poster.
6. Explain that bee also rolls in flower, combs and scrapes its body for pollen, then stores it in between hairs on back legs (pollen baskets).

7. Show "Bee's Pollen Baskets" poster and explain that bees carry pollen home in pollen baskets.

Teacher Demonstration
1. Tell students they will make paper flowers with pollen.
2. Identify parts of real flower.
3. Demonstrate making flower while comparing paper parts to real parts (see page 19).
4. Cut snips in piece of green paper for grass.
5. Glue grass to base of flower.

Children Make Flowers
1. Have children go to tables and make flowers.
2. Remind them to write names on back of blossoms.
3. Distribute paper for stamens, pollen, and grass.
4. Have children place or tape flowers on mural. (Do not use glue).

Session 2: Nectar

Nectar Sippers
1. Show "Bee's Proboscis" poster. Ask, "What do you think a bee would do with a mouth shaped like a straw?"
2. Explain that bees suck sweet juice called nectar, using a straw-like mouthpiece called a proboscis.
3. Hand out straws and paper cups of juice. Have children pretend to be bees sucking nectar.
4. Explain that nectar is turned to honey in a special stomach—a honey stomach.
5. Ask, "Why do you think a bee makes honey?" Encourage all responses while explaining that bees eat honey.
6. Hand out honey on waxed paper for students to taste.

Reviewing
Bring class together to review proboscis, nectar, and pollen.

Lesson 3: Building A Beehive

Discovering the Hive
1. Explain that many animals like honey. Ask, "Do any of you know where bees hide their honey?"
2. Show "Beehives" and "Inside the Hive" posters. Point out honeycomb.

3. Explain that small, empty spaces are called cells. Ask, "Do any of you know what these cells are made of?"
4. Hold up wax. Ask what people make from wax. Display wax objects.

Adding Wax Scales

1. Show "Bee With Wax Scales" poster. Discuss how bees make wax and ask on which body section the wax scales appear.
2. Show children how to make bee with wax scales (see instructions on page 30).
3. Have children take their bees from mural to work area.
4. Have children add wax scales to bees.

Joining Bees in Building a Hive

1. Have students bring bees to discussion area and arrange bees in straight lines, with wax scales showing.
2. Display "Bees Hanging in Chains" poster.
3. Explain how and why bees hang in chains.
4. Have children pretend their bees are hanging in chains. Demonstrate with three bees to show how they actually hang, not lie flat.
5. Suggest class join bees in building hive.
   a. Hold up empty egg carton, saying "Let's pretend these are cells a paper bee made."
   b. Cut lid off carton.
   c. Write your name on side of carton to show students where to write their names.
   d. Holding up nearby paper bee, explain that bee places wax scale on cell of hive. Remove a scale.
   e. Glue scale(s) to egg carton cell.
6. Pass out or have children pick up egg cartons and take to work area.
7. Have children make cells for hive.
8. Spread out large paper hive in discussion area. Have children place cells and bees inside hive, explaining that many bees work together to build hive.
9. Ask students not to glue or tape cells to hive, because in next session they will remove cells and fill them, after learning what bees put in them.

Reflecting

As children sit around paper hive, ask, "What surprised you about a beehive?" Spend a few minutes sharing thoughts.

Lesson 4: What's In A Hive?

Session 1: Exploring Honeycomb

Exploring Honeycomb

1. For review, ask what the cells are made of [Wax.] and introduce real honeycomb saying, "Let's find out what bees put in the wax cells."
2. Pass uncut honeycomb around. Point out how wax is used to cap cells filled with honey.
3. Distribute small honeycomb pieces on waxed paper for children to taste.

Session 2: The Queen Bee and Her Babies

The Queen Bee

1. Gather students in discussion area.
2. Ask, "What do bees hide in the wax cells inside the hive?" Explain that in addition to honey, eggs are also hidden there.
3. Ask, "Does anyone know the name of the bee that lays all of the eggs?"
4. Walk paper queen bee out of hive. Ask, "What bee is this?" [Queen.]
5. Compare queen with demonstration bee, asking why she is so much larger than the other bees. Explain that the queen is fed a special food called **royal jelly**.
6. Show "The Queen Bee and Her Eggs" poster. Notice the eggs and huge abdomen.

Baby Bees and Nurse Bees

1. Tell class that when baby bees first hatch they are small, white, and worm-like, and are called **larvae**. One baby bee is called a larva.
2. Show "The Larvae" poster. Have student point out larvae and nurse bee. Explain that nurse bees feed royal jelly to larvae when they first hatch.
3. Explain that older larvae eat **bee bread**.
4. Explain how bees make bee bread.
    a. Hold up tray with cups. Have children pretend cups are honeycomb cells. Show cup of honey.
    b. Remind children about pollen baskets and ask where bees hide pollen. Show graham cracker crumbs (pretend pollen) hidden in cup (pretend cell).
    c. Mix small amount of crumbs with honey.
    d. Explain that honey mixed with pollen is bee bread.

5. Role-play baby bees and nurse bees.
   a. Give straw and cup with honey to every other child: they are nurse bees.
   b. Sprinkle crumbs in cups for nurse bees to mix with honey.
   c. Have nurse bees feed baby bees with straw used as spoon.
   d. Afterward, nurse bees discard straws and cups.
   e. Reverse roles and pass out straws and cups to new nurse bees.

Change to Adult Bee

1. Explain that larvae eat and grow, filling up the cells. Then something exciting happens.
2. Show students "The Pupae" poster.
   a. Have them note darkness of cells. Explain that worker bees covered cells with wax.
   b. Point out **cocoon**. Explain that larvae have made cocoons and changed to **pupae**.
   c. Have students compare changes they see.
   d. If age appropriate, explain that this change from egg to larva to pupa to adult bee is called **metamorphosis**.
3. Place "The Larvae" and "The Pupae" posters side by side and have students observe and compare.

Teacher Demonstration

1. Gather children around paper hive and have them discuss things that are hidden in real wax cells. Ask, "What could we put in the cells?" [Eggs, baby bees.]
2. Cut white paper in quarters. Draw egg, larva, pupa on separate pieces and glue paper in cells.
3. Ask, "What else is kept in cells in a hive?" [Honey, pollen.]
Pretend brown paper is honey, and yellow paper is pollen. Cut into quarters and paste one each in separate cells. To make bee bread, paste yellow and brown pieces in one cell.

Children Fill Their Egg Carton Cells

1. Have children get their egg cartons and fill with paper honey, pollen, bee bread, eggs, larvae, pupae.
2. Have them place egg carton cells inside large hive.

Session 3: Young Bees Drama

Young Bees Drama
1. Have the children pretend to be sleepy adult bees who have just chewed their way out of their cells. Have them walk lazily to circle and sit down quietly. Ask, "What do you think the sleepy young bees do after they chew their way out of their cells?"
2. Expose inside of hive, showing sleepy bees.
3. Dramatize bee behavior while describing life stages.
    a. Keeping bees warm in cells.
    b. Feeding bee bread to larvae.
    c. Taking care of, cleaning, and feeding royal jelly to the queen.
    d. Producing wax for building cells.
    e. Fanning wings to cool hive.
4. Explain that young bees work inside hive, while older, stronger bees fly out to flowers, gathering nectar and pollen.
5. As you hand out bees, have children decide if they want their bees to be young or old.
6. Have those who choose older bees:
    a. fly bees to mural, to collect nectar and pollen.
    b. leave bees on flowers.
    c. return to the circle.
7. Have those who choose young bees:
    a. decide what jobs their bees should do inside hive.
    b. take turns telling class what their bee is doing while arranging bee on comb doing its job.

Lesson 5: Bee Enemies

Bee Enemies
1. Read text on page 57 or make up similar story.
2. Introduce the word **predator**. Have students name bee predators.

Teacher Demonstration
1. Ask, "What does a skunk eat?" Have children share general knowledge about skunks.
2. Show students how to make a paper skunk (see instructions on pages 57, 58).

Children Make Paper Skunks
1. Direct children to tables to make paper skunks.
2. Have them write their names on undersides of paper skunks.

Role-Playing Guard Bees
1. Gather students in discussion area. Walk paper skunk to hive. Ask, "What do you think would happen if a skunk wandered over to a beehive?" Discuss.
2. Explain that guard bees stay near doorway of hive. They are middle-aged, the strongest, they attack when enemies threaten. Ask, "How would bees attack an enemy?" [Sting it.] Explain that one way bees detect enemies is through scent. Ask, "What do bees have to help them smell an enemy?" [Antennae.]
3. Give scented cottonball to each child.
4. Choose several students to be guard bees while rest of class leaves room. Guard bees stand in doorway and as other children try to enter they check scent.
5. Ask what would happen if a bee from another hive tried to enter.

Protection
1. Discuss with class ways that people are protected.
2. Ask how bees are protected from rain and cold weather.
3. Have class snuggle together to feel warmth.
4. Explain that young bees fan wings to cool hive.
5. Have children fan themselves and each other.

Lesson 6: Bee School, Beelines, and Bee Dances

Bee's Age

1. In discussion area, explain that you can tell a bee's age by the job it is doing. Ask what young bees do.
2. Ask what middle-aged bees do. [Guard hive.]
3. Explain that as bee gets older its wings grow stronger and it can fly farther. Ask, "What job do you think these bees do? [Gather nectar and pollen.]

Paper Pollen

1. For review, show "Bee Covered with Pollen," and "Bee's Pollen Baskets" posters.
2. Tell class that all paper bees are now old enough to fly to flowers and collect nectar and pollen.
3. Demonstrate gluing yellow paper pollen to bee's back legs.
4. Have children get their bees, go to work area, and glue on paper pollen.
5. Have them fly bees to paper flowers and pretend bees are collecting pollen.

Bee School

1. Explain that before bees go out for pollen and nectar, they need to go to "bee school" to learn to find way back to hive. Say, "Let's go to our bee school."
2. Go outside. Find place for pretend beeh such as side of building.
3. Have children face building, and explain that bees fly backwards, looking at hive to remember what it looks like.
   a. Have students walk backwards away from hive, stopping several times to note landmarks.
   b. Explain that bees also use the sun to help them find way back.
   c. Ask if students feel sun on backs, faces, or sides. Have them walk toward hive, making sure they still feel sun where they felt it before.

Beelines

1. Explain that when bees gather nectar and pollen, they fly in straight line called a **beeline**.
2. Have students try walking in straight line. Then have them try running in straight line.
3. Tell students bees also fly home in a beeline, after collecting nectar and pollen.

Bee Dances

1. Ask, "How do you think a bee would tell the other bees about nectar and pollen?" During discussion, explain that bees do two dances to do this.
2. If flowers are nearby, bees do a round dance:
    a. Demonstrate by walking in a large circle, moving arms (wings) up and down rapidly.
    b. Tell students wings make a loud, whirring noise. When other bees hear it, they join dance.
    c. Encourage children to join dance.
    d. Explain that as soon as bees understand the message, they make a beeping sound and fly to flowers. Have children "fly" to flowers.
3. Move flowers farther away (100 feet or more).
4. Explain that bees do figure-eight dance when flowers are far away. If very far away, bees act tired and move slowly. Demonstrate bee's movements as you explain.
    a. Tell children that bee starts dance facing in direction of flowers in center of figure-eight.
    b. Also called the waggle dance because bees wiggle abdomen in center of figure-eight. Wiggling sends off more flower scent.
    c. Complete a figure-eight, wiggling in center.
    d. When students understand message, have them beep and "fly" with you toward flowers.
5. Move the flowers. Have a student role-play the dancing bee. Repeat activity.
6. Hide flowers. Have one child watch where hidden, and communicate the direction to others with the waggle dance.

Communicating

1. Review messages bees communicate in dances [Scent, direction, distance of flowers.]

2. Discuss ways people communicate nonverbally.

   a. What does a policeman do when he wants you to stop your car?

   b. What do parents do when they want you to quiet down?

   c. What does it mean when someone shakes head back and forth? Up and down?

3. Suggest students notice ways people communicate with each other using hands, heads, faces, and other parts of body.

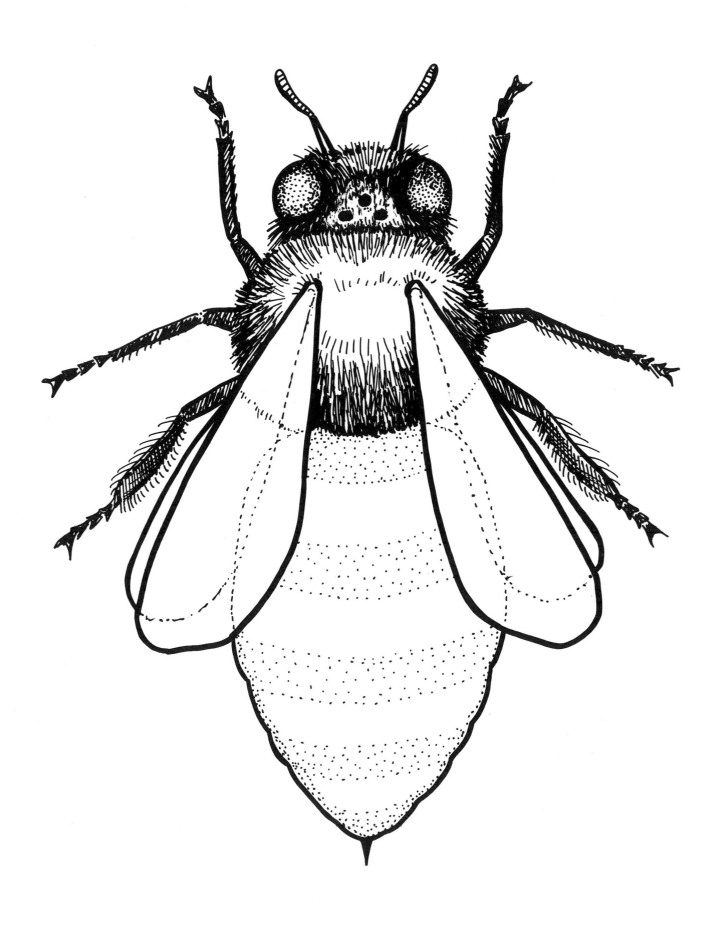

THE HONEYBEE

BEE COVERED WITH
POLLEN

Great Explorations in Math and Science: *Buzzing a Hive*

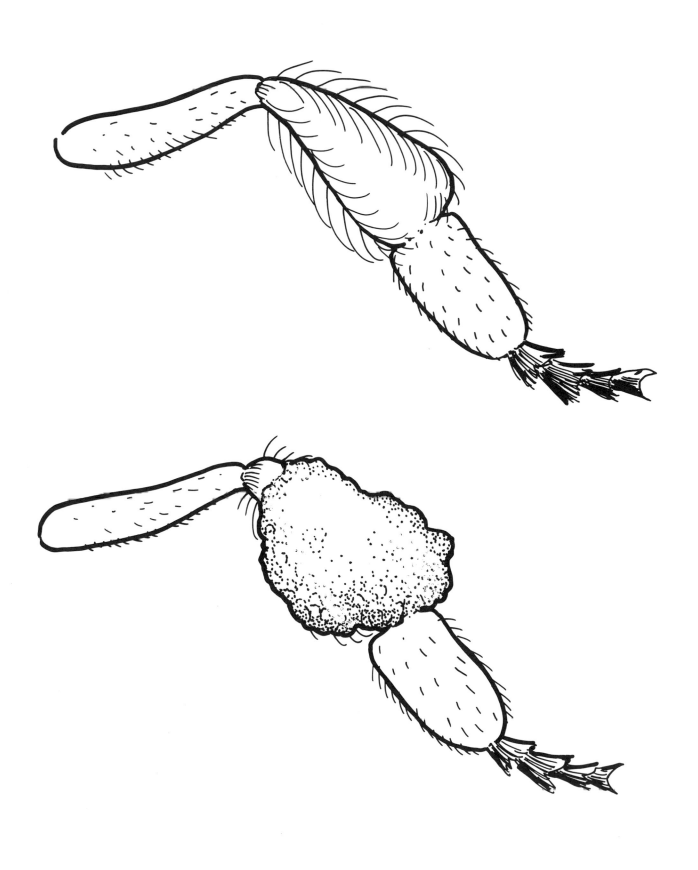

BEE'S POLLEN BASKETS

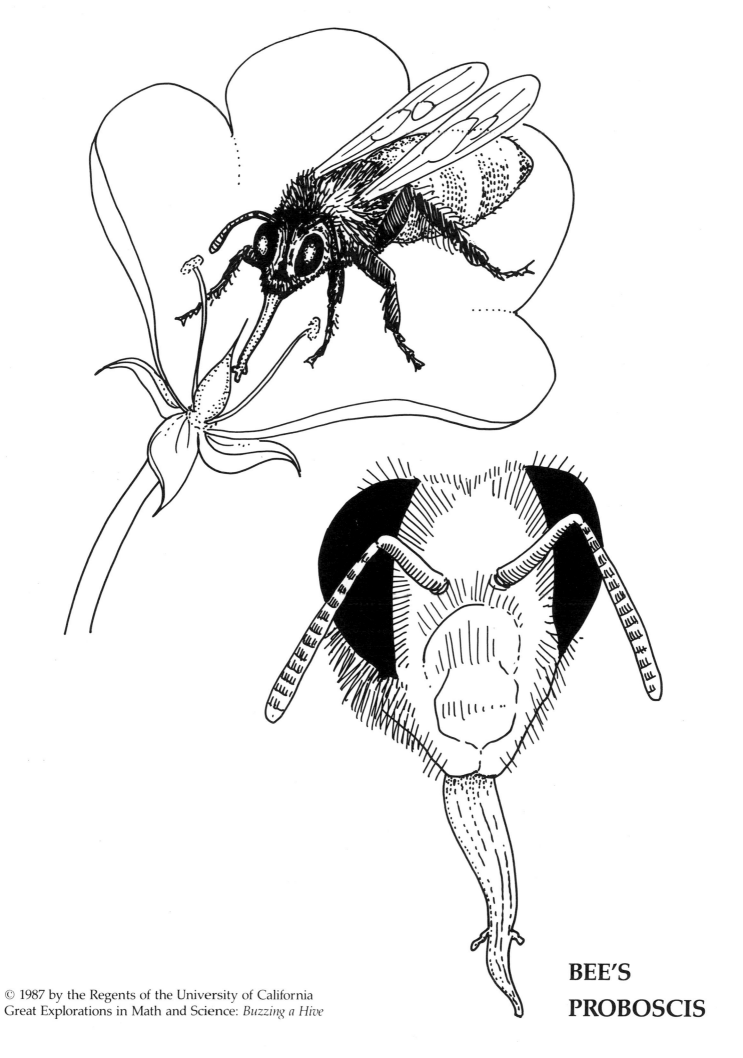

BEE'S

PROBOSCIS

Straw Hive

Wooden Hive

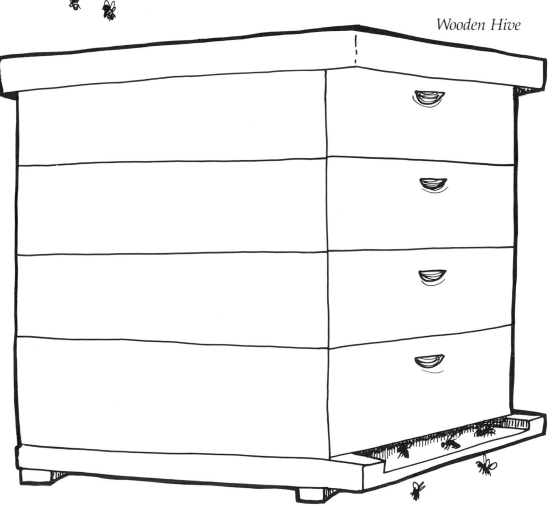

BEEHIVES

Great Explorations in Math and Science: *Buzzing a Hive*

INSIDE
THE HIVE

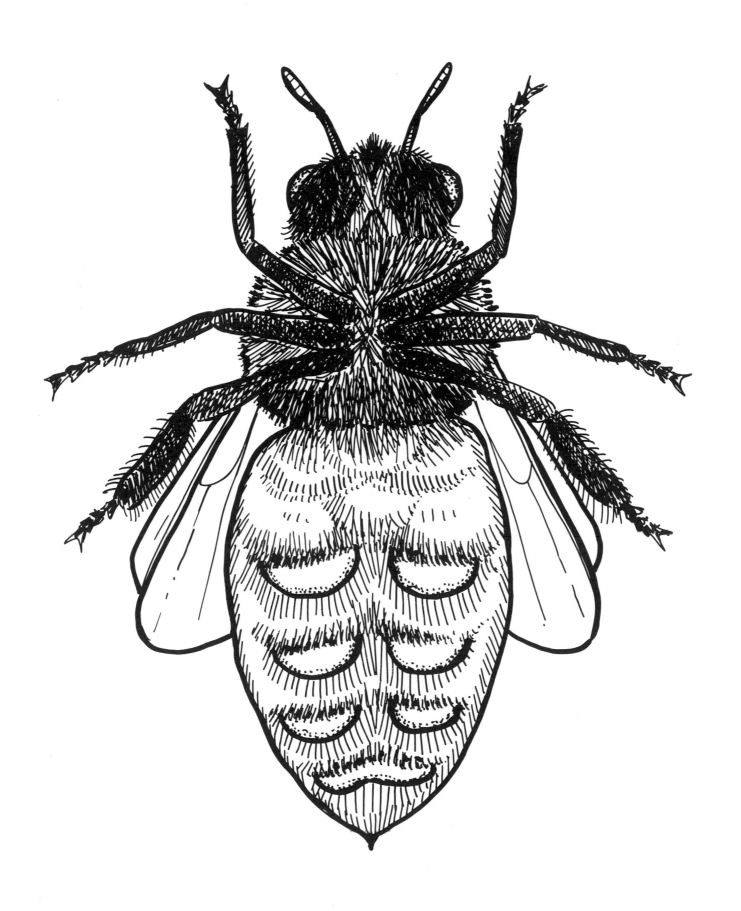

BEE WITH WAX SCALES

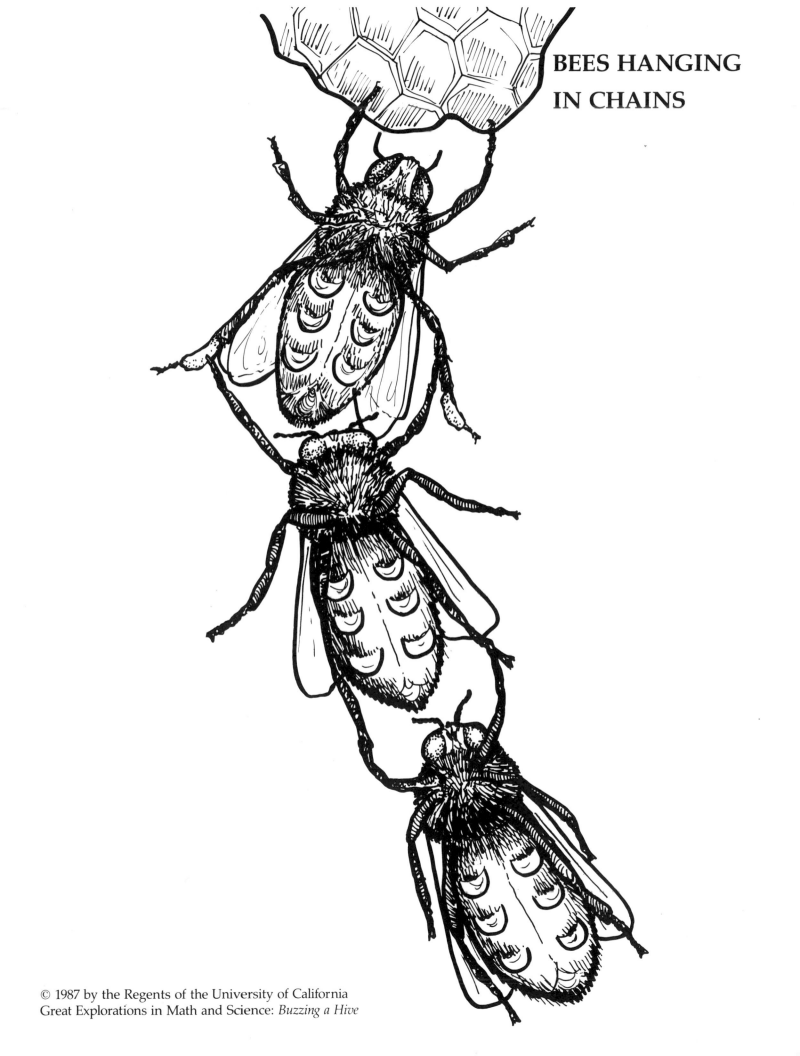

BEES HANGING
IN CHAINS

THE QUEEN BEE AND HER EGGS

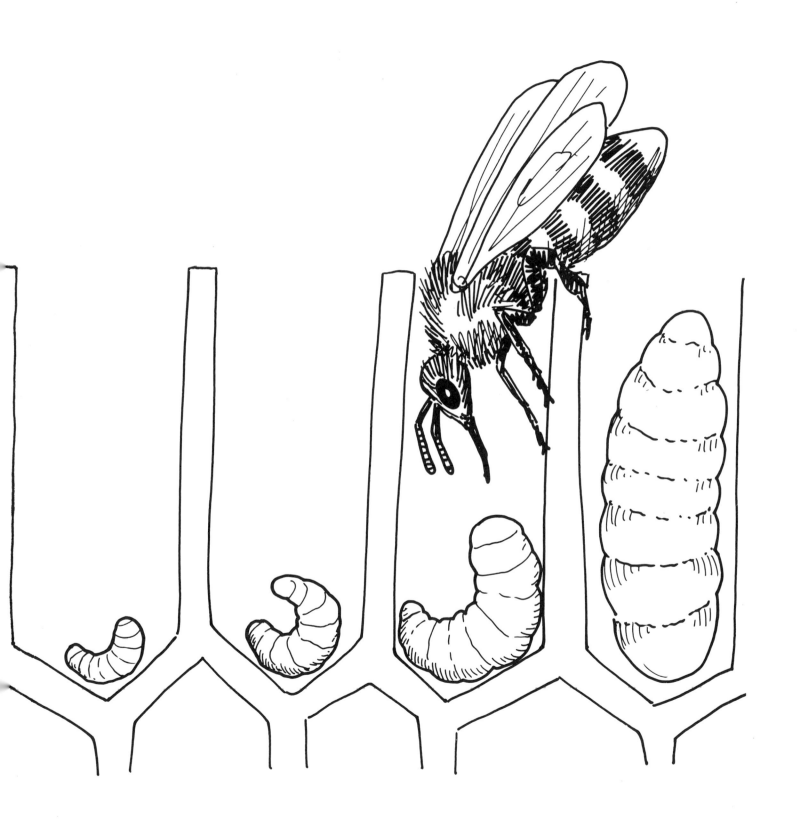

THE LARVAE

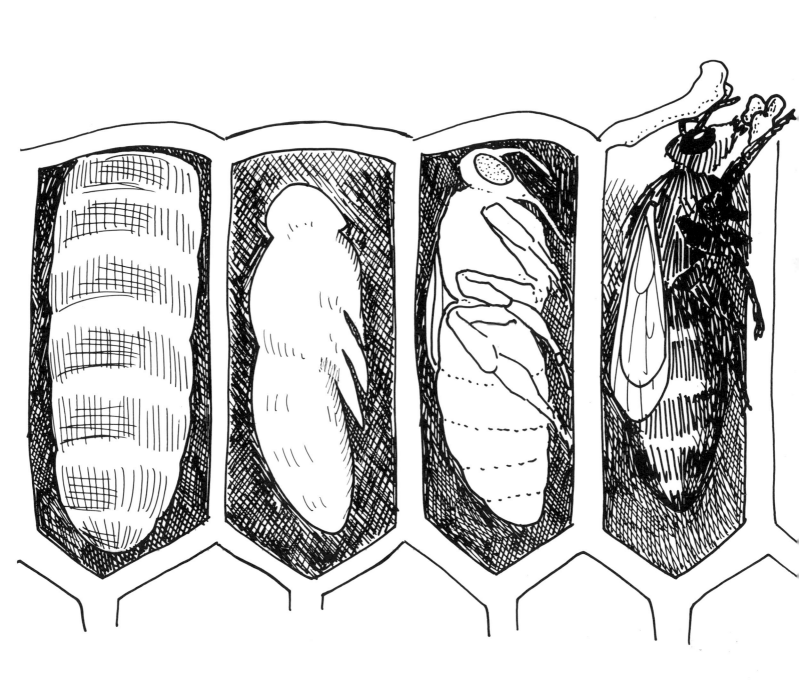

THE PUPAE